# MY EARNEST EXPECTATIONS

## ANCHORED IN LOVE

### AS ENDLESS AS THE SEA

By
R.D. MILLUS

All scripture is from the King James Holy Bible, New King James Holy Bible, and New International Version unless otherwise quoted, therefore, quoted as written.

My Earnest Expectations

Copyright © 2024 by R.D. Millus

Published by R.D. Millus

Edited by R.D. Millus

Printed and bound in the United States of America, all rights reserved. Active 1: The publisher prohibits the reproduction or transmission of any part of this publication in any form or by any means, including electronic, mechanical, or digital methods, except for brief passages quoted by a reviewer in a magazine, newspaper, or on the web, without written permission from the publisher.

For further information or to purchase additional copies of this book or other books by this author, please contact,

Rdmmillus55@yahoo.com

https://www.amazon.com/stores/R.-D.MILLUS/author/B09NFHRC2Q

ISBN: 979-889397-0500

LCCN:

# DEDICATION AND ACKNOWLEDGMENTS

I dedicate this book to those who struggle with being misled into believing that they should be ashamed or discouraged due to the difficulties of this life. Jesus equips those whom He calls. As believers, we are one body with many parts, and God has ordained each individual with a gift or gifts and talents fitted to each according to their ability. Jesus sent the Holy Spirit to dwell within those who have confessed and believed that He died to forgive us of our sins and that God raised Him from the grave after three days, therefore defeating spiritual death.

I give my thanks and my love to Anna Marie Millus, my wife and best friend, for her love and support for over 31 years, and to Dr. William Galloska, pastor and friend on behalf of his solid doctrinal teaching on the Word of God, and JoEllen Claypool, editor, and book coach for her patience in correcting my errors.

When we think about the modern confines of prison, we should understand that in Paul's day, a jail cell represented a place of torment and sometimes loneliness. Our modern prison system, though dangerous, contains many of the modern comforts of home. A cell such as this one is where Paul penned many of his letters. So, he was no stranger to prison cells. Some believe it was fitting for him to spend time in a place where he had sent so many of Jesus' followers before Jesus blinded him on the Damascus road. We should understand that though the sizes of the cells are roughly the same as many modern prison cells of today, many of these cells were open to the outside elements. To the glory of God go the wonderful results from such a time spent and the number of lost souls touched by the Apostle Paul when confined behind bars.

# FORWARD

Philippians chapter 1 lends philosophy to the Christian life. Paul ascribes this epistle to him in that he associates his name to that of Timothy; in his view, both are "servants" or bond slaves to our Lord Jesus Christ.

We read in the Scripture the term "Grace" (charis), which is the Greek form of salutation; and "peace" (Shalom) is the Hebrew for greeting. One writer puts it this way. "We must know the grace of God before we can experience the peace of God." Is he correct? Can we not admit that grace is the purity of love in action? Knowing the grace of God and living as in the grace of God is all-inclusive unto the peace of God. I do not believe we can separate them unless we are indulging in temporal worldly separation, meaning we are sustaining one foot in the body and the other in the temporal satisfaction of worldly indulgence.

To separate the two, one must determine which lifestyle is more beneficial for his or her desire to become a Christian. How will Christ view the conversion upon returning to His bride? Will He find purity? This is a daunting question to one who wants to taste the peace of God yet remains on the fringe of the worldly aspects of life. Therefore, what is the most earnest expectation of the believer in such a lifestyle? Are there any aspects of a Christian life that would cause one to be ashamed of the Gospel or one's existence?

# TABLE OF CONTENTS

CHAPTER 1 ..........................................................................................1
   BE NOT ASHAMED ........................................................................1

CHAPTER 2 ........................................................................................10
   OBJECT OF PERCEPTION ............................................................10

CHAPTER 3 ........................................................................................16
   THE VISION OF OBEDIENCE ........................................................16

CHAPTER 4 ........................................................................................26
   THE POWER OF GOD UNTO SALVATION....................................26

CHAPTER 5 ........................................................................................32
   FAITH CREATES CHANGE ............................................................32

CHAPTER 6 ........................................................................................38
   YIELDING TO CHRIST ....................................................................38

CHAPTER 7 ........................................................................................41
   YIELDING TO GOD'S PURPOSE ..................................................41

CHAPTER 8 ........................................................................................49
   YIELDING TO THE CALL OF GOD................................................49

CHAPTER 9 ........................................................................................52
   THE ORDINANCES OF GOD'S CALLING....................................52

CHAPTER 10 ......................................................................................55
   BELIEF IN CHRIST, WHAT IT IS TO ME ......................................55

CHAPTER 11 ......................................................................................59
   CHRISTIANS CALLING FOR UNITY..............................................59

CHAPTER 12 ......................................................................................76
   HOW LONG LORD? ......................................................................76

INVITATION ........................................................................................82

ABOUT THE AUTHOR ..................................................................... 83
BIBLIOGRAPHY ............................................................................... 84

# CHAPTER 1

## BE NOT ASHAMED

"According to my earnest expectations and my hope, that in nothing I shall be ashamed, but *that with* all boldness, as always, *so* now also Christ shall be magnified in my body, whether *it be* by life or by death," (KJV, Phil. 1:20).

Paul's eagerness and his desire in life is that he would not be ashamed of his testimony in Christ. The apostle was ever conscious of his witness and his teaching of the Gospel because he wished not to be ashamed of his service when he came into the presence of Jesus Christ. Therefore, is it implying that believers may be ashamed of having a weak witness when our Lord returns for His Church?

Therefore, can we agree, that it is possible that even though so many saved people talk about the coming of Christ again earnestly, they are unwilling to admit they are not ready for it or the possibility that they will feel ashamed of their witness and it looms large in their heart? Should we not be concerned about that conviction in our hearts as a believer?

Should we give thought to our most earnest expectations, as did the Apostle Paul in his letter to the Philippians? At some point, the apostle knew he would come before Christ and give an account for his service to God. Do we think about such actions? We will one day die, save for those in the rapture.

**"For to me to live is Christ, and to die *is* gain," (KJV, Phil. 1:21).**

Philippians 1:1 represents Paul's thanks and love for the Saints, overseers, and deacons in Christ Jesus. Verse 21 declares his mission in life, which is to glorify Christ. The Christian's mission in life ought to be centered on glorifying our Lord and Savior Christ Jesus. Paul's entire consecration is to Christ, his love for the Church, and Spiritual joy. Verse 20 lends merit to Paul's motivation, which depicts Christ as being magnified in his body, either in life or death. Paul's philosophy of life lends credence to his belief that to live is to serve Christ, and to die is to gain eternal life.

Therefore, what is the genuine test of a saint's life's actions? Is it based on successfulness or faithfulness as the measure of one's life in connection to the human level of life? Our human relationships are the same conditions in which we should exhibit an ideal life in Christ. Amen.

**"Whether therefore ye eat, or drink, or whatsoever ye do, do all to the glory of God," (KJV, 1 Cor. 10:31).**

I pondered this question: "Is the most important thing in my life as a Christian the reality of Jesus Christ in my life?" It's not too farfetched to understand the necessity of serving the Lord; however, is it not more the talk about being dedicated and having a heartfelt desire to serve Him than it is an action? Is it not possible to locate within what we, as an individual, are most passionate about? Is it serving Christ?

Look at the ant, always busy doing what is required individually for the overall service to the collective purpose of the larger body. For the ant, it is about survival. For the human serving God, it is about sharing the Gospel and fellowship above all else. Everything else falls under the heading of the fruit that flows from having fellowship with Him, resulting in an absorbed witness for Christ in a wilderness of lost souls. "But if I live in the flesh, this is the fruit of my labour: yet what shall I choose I wot not," (KJV, Phil. 1:22).

Like Paul, we know little about the future. Only a fool believes he knows, without a doubt, what the next second of life shall bring. The word "wot" is present tense; it means "God knows." We may want to say and believe that we have experienced a wonderful call from

God. Therefore, how do we display that call to others in everyday life? Making a statement without action is empty.

**"Even as I please all *men* in all *things*, not seeking my own profit, but the *profit* of many, that they may be saved," (KJV, 1 Cor. 10:33).**

I read a story about a preacher who asked his congregation who wanted to go to heaven. Everyone raised their hands except one small boy. The preacher asked him, "Son, don't you want to go to Heaven?" The boy's response was, "I sure do, but I thought you were getting up a load for tonight."

To be honest, do we not all want to go to Heaven, but not right now? Paul had the desire to leave this life; however, God placed him among these people to lead them to Christ. God's purpose for Paul was not complete, hence, it was not his time.

**"And hope maketh not ashamed; because the love of God is shed abroad in our hearts by the Holy Ghost which is given unto us," (KJV, Rom. 5:5).**

In verse 5:4, the apostle Paul presents a challenging concept that Christians can find joy in suffering, and thus the hope of true believers should not be ashamed. Paul is writing his epistle from the confines of prison. Let us be clear, though, the apostle never intended that anyone should feel happy or enthusiastic under the pressures of suffering. His elementary thought here is that our faith in Christ provides us the grace and strength to not only rejoice as we travel through all situations, be they good or bad, but rejoice in the knowledge that we are worthwhile to our loving Father, by growing into the person our Loving Father intended us to become. Jesus sent the Holy Spirit to dwell within those who accepted His great sacrifice on the cross. Some claim that the apostle's statement is the most powerful benefit mentioned. (Compare Rom. 5:1-11).

**"And now dear children, continue in him, so that when he appears, we may be confident and unashamed before him at his coming. If you know that he is righteous, you know that everyone that does what is right has been born of him," (New International Version, 1 Jn. 2:28-29).**

Verse 28 suggests that if we do not yield to Jesus those areas of our life which He has asked us to yield, and our determined purpose is to be the greatest for His highest, should our best therefore, bring glory to Him? Will my stubborn pride cause my best to be tainted? Let us be honest; we live in a prideful, modern, I-can-do-this-myself world. We must shed our prideful hearts before coming into His Holy presence; otherwise, we merely spit words into the wind.

Pay attention. Is it not by the absolute and irrevocable surrender of the will, meaning at that point, I have determined to be absolutely and entirely for Him and Him alone? Our ever-changing world, with its constant bombardment of worldly distractions, makes it challenging to answer the question? The simple truth of modern society is that people are self-indulged, self-governed, self-satisfied, and self-spirited, etc.

Experience has taught me that my human way of thinking includes an undue amount of thought and consideration for myself, hindering my ability to reach that level of complete and utter dependence upon Jesus. I honestly must admit that I have covered it up by the pretense that, I am doing it for others, clinging to that small amount of selfishness not yet yielded to Jesus. Ponder this question: would that small amount of selfishness reserved deep within your heart cause you to be a little ashamed if Jesus suddenly appeared? Is it worth thinking about? YES.

**"For whosoever shall be ashamed of me and my words, of him shall the Son of man be ashamed, when he shall come in his own glory, and *in his* Father's, and of the holy angels," (KJV, Luke 9:26).**

Should we not be continually aware that Jesus knows our hearts, and that He knows our level of confidence in Him? Humans are experts in hiding things from each other; however, we cannot hide anything from Christ. Self-preservation lives in our human nature, which is not necessarily bad until it crosses paths with the will of our Father in Heaven. Our purpose is to serve God by sharing what God has freely given unto us through His Son, Jesus Christ. History proves that God blesses those who earnestly desire to seek His will in their lives.

Now, watch this; if we were to give serious thought about what it may or may not cost others around us when we openly obey the call of God, do I dare tell God that He doesn't know what my obedience will mean or what it might cost me or those around me? It is an honest question, yet arrogant because even though we call ourselves devout believers in Christ; there may be a few who do not honestly desire to see another's salvation take place. Read the story of Jonah and you will find the concept of such a thought is not far off our thought patterns. Honestly, is it not human nature to want justice? And do we not want God or the authority in charge to bring hard judgment upon those who have wronged us? However, it may flicker in our thoughts for a moment that we want justice and the authority to punish those who have wronged us.

We must not follow through with our judgmental thoughts, allowing them to fester and become actions of destruction in another's life or our own. **"...vengeance *is* mine; I will repay, saith the Lord. Therefore if thine enemy hunger, feed him; if he thirst, give him drink: for in so doing thou shalt heap coals of fire on his head,"** (KJV, Rom. 12:19-20).

Paul is saying we should not place ourselves on God's throne of judgment and do all things within the boundaries of love. There are no righteous expectations in a revengeful heart and so when we try to place ourselves as the judge and executioner of judgment, <u>we shall</u> face the consequences of our actions because pain and heartache follow destruction. The trickle-down effects of a revengeful heart give birth to destruction not unlike a river of lava that flows, spreading in all directions, maybe even unto the death of the one judged. Only a cold, hateful heart would relish such results. Destruction bleeds destruction, therefore, is it possible to be the judge of others yet believe we earnestly expect God to say, "Well done thy good and faithful servant?" Would that not be a prideful belief?

Therefore, we are to keep ourselves before God, keeping in mind that our highest level of obedience is entirely for Him and Him alone. "There, but for the grace of God go I." This is an expression that is used to convict one's heart to admit that one cannot judge another for their flaws, for in the eyes of God, we are all equally flawed. Amen. (Read 2 Cor. 15:8-10). Some say they attributed this expression to a man named John Bradford, who quoted it upon watching a group of prisoners being led to execution in the year 1553. Two years later, they executed Bradford for heresy. He was a protestant living under Roman Catholic English.

Take hold of this thought by Oswald Chambers, "Our unstoppable determination for His Holiness" means that even in life or death, it makes no difference. In simple terms: In or out, there is no in-between with the Holiness of God.

**"Beloved, if our heart does not condemn us, we have confidence toward God," (NKJV, 1 Jn. 3:21).**

The Apostle Paul was determined that nothing would stop him from doing exactly what God called him to do. Paul was a man of perseverance witnessed by his actions in his earlier days as Saul seeking to destroy the "Way Movement" (Christianity). He believed with all his heart that he was doing the will of God. Even though

Jesus had ascended back to Heaven, Jesus knew the heart of Saul, and that his attitude and perseverance were misguided by the historical misinterpretation of the Law. Paul was devout in what he believed according to the Law, and his devotion to God.

Jesus needed to redirect Saul's mindset and change it. He did that on the Damascus road. The glorious light of the Lord brought Saul to a level of obedience, meaning the lowest point that he had ever encountered. When Paul reached his lowest point, he had to rely completely on others since his complete blindness crushed his self-will. This is the point we reach when all else has failed. It creates a void and surrounds that void with a fear of the unknown. Our little dog lost ninety-nine percent of his sight and hearing. He walks around with his head down wondering why we no longer talk to him. Only Christ can fill that void in us and remove that unknown fear. Lowliness of mind and consideration of others will produce happier and sounder relationships. Remember, the abundance of the heart creates action. The action may be positive or negative concerning one's salvation.

I believe as others; that strife and selfish vainness and pride lead to the division of church and families. Do we not look for wonder in our experiences and do we not mistake heroic actions for authentic heroes? We live in a culture that thrives on the heroic actions of others, even though cartoon characters created to feed that hunger, and/or bank accounts, and the images produced result in false hopes.

Ponder this thought. It's one thing to go through a storm or a crisis of life grandly; however, it is quite different to face that crisis or everyday life glorifying God when there is no witness, no limelight, and no one paying even the remotest of attention to our ordeals. When we recognize the absolute freedom that surrounds knowledge and action yielding all things to Christ. Is that not far better than being in bondage to the self-indulgence of an empty and temporal journey that shall end in darkness?

Jesus removed Saul's physical sight, and that action brought him to a whole new level of dependence, which he had never encountered before. Saul's confidence in what he perceived to be the work of God brought him face-to-face with his human arrogance. Saul is a highly educated man in the law, and the Pharisees and Sadducees placed high praise for his education as did the Roman Empire, at least, to a certain point for his commitment to wiping out that which the Jews perceived to be blasphemy against God, (Christianity).

The Roman Empire could have cared less about Jesus. However, Jesus was causing strife among the Jews up to the point the Jews empowered the ruling government (Rome) to get involved. In today's world, God's Word is causing strife among the ruling parties that want God out of the picture. Is it, not the elitists and/or socialists doing their very best to rid the world of Christ?

The same came against Paul in his journeys to spread the gospel. We are called by God to spread the Gospel. It is far better to be unnoticed by others knowing that God's Spirit is in us, making us completely His to a point at which we do not seek to gain vain attention, Amen.

Speaking from experience, I once lived a vain lifestyle. Not to the point of wanting to hurt others' feelings on purpose, however, I was so self-indulged that I cared little for the feelings of others. My actions centered on satisfying my desires of the flesh, pushing me into areas that brought unintended results and heartache. After getting married and having children, I felt my fleshly desires decrease, not disappear, but become less important. I realized that my parent's influence on the importance of family became more prevalent. Even though I was fighting the uphill battle of siblings condemning me to the level of being worthless, I looked at their lifestyle, and it turned out we were the same. A co-worker kept inviting me to church. One night, I went forward and accepted Christ into my heart. That old selfish nature fought back hard. However, my God is bigger than the fleshly beast that continues to pound on the door, demanding attention. If you believe it cannot happen to you, then stop and think about what the worldly flesh is pushing on your children in public schools and public media. Cartoons are indoctrinating young minds to believe alternative lifestyles are good. God asserts that SIN IS NOT FINE and that it is an abomination in direct disobedience to Himself.

# CHAPTER 2

## OBJECT OF PERCEPTION

The objects of perception are the entities we attend to as to the when and what we perceive of the world. Some believe that perception lies at the root of all our empirical knowledge. A great deal of knowledge comes through testimony, but our original knowledge is based on perceiving the world through our five senses: hearing, tasting, seeing, touching, and smelling. Therefore, as one writer put it; "Perception may be of a great theory of knowledge about a branch of philosophy which entails the study of nature, origins and the limits of human knowledge." An explanation of empirical knowledge is,

**1.** In philosophy, we gain knowledge from experience rather than from innate ideas or deductive reasoning.

**2.** Scientists gain knowledge in the sciences through experiments and observation, not theory.

As an illustration, what is the fundamental question on which we base our perception? My research depicted that:

**1.** Now, pastors, may possess a theological or Biblical perspective, a problem-solving method more than likely picked up in a seminary.

**2.** From a Biblical perspective, some claim that we serve a God of justice. Is God a God of justice? Yes, He is and Scripture proves it in the past, our present, and our future, which is based on His coming judgment of sin, and for all the wrongs committed in the history of humanity; justice shall be served, and righteousness will prevail, amen.

**3.** A particular perspective is a way of thinking about something, especially one that is influenced by beliefs or experiences.

**4.** The Christian perception of perfection lies in the rendering of several Hebrew and Greek words in which the fundamental idea of perfection is that of completeness. However, let us not forget that perfection is an attribute of God alone, meaning that at His highest He is alone, He is complete, wanting nothing as in His perfection is eternal with no possibility of defect. This is an impossible attribute, that which we, as sin-natured humans, cannot attain this side of Heaven.

Personal experience has taught me that even Christians can become arrogant, even in our duty to God. Therefore, I believe the devil is lurking around every corner awaiting the right opportunity to strike a blow upon my witness. Our actions before conversion were on full display to those around us. A simple truth that we may overlook is the devil also is aware of our sin before conversion, and he will store-front that sin to tempt us after conversion. Those around us may shower us with praise for a task completed for the Body of Christ. We may believe that is a good thing, which is to be recognized by our peers; however, we must learn to temper that praise by being alert to our ego's ability to slide to the front of all things important. However, it may start as a small thing, and we must learn to recognize it. It is at that point, our witness may take a hit and cause another weaker brother or sister to stumble. We can temper the praise with the truth of God's Word and an attitude of believing God is working through us for His purpose and not from our self-inflicted desires of the flesh.

Our communion with God factors in our gracious regard toward Him and His gracious regard toward us. A good example is that of Abraham and the communion that occurred between him and God, which rested in the providence and the ordinances of God concerning the events at Sodom. The meeting between God and Abraham before Sodom's destruction depicts the purpose of keeping up the providence, as well as the ordinance of God.

Abraham had a pious regard for God concerning Sodom. Abraham arose early and looked toward Sodom. For what purpose? He watched from the point where he had welcomed the three visitors. Abraham's concern for Sodom depicts the heart of Abraham toward others.

When we have prayed, is it not wise to look after our prayers and observe the results of them?

Now, the flip side of this coin represents those who are unresponsive to God's gentle nudges. Does He not bring us to the place where He asks us to take the next step to a higher level of trust in Him? Is it not at that point that we may sense fear, allowing our minds to join the debate? I believe we are motivated by our perception, but God's truth motivates us spiritually. Here is a hard truth. When we engage in a debate with God, He may create a crisis that forces us to decide either for or against His purpose for our life (Acts 9:3-5). Stop and think about whether you are in crisis. If the answer is yes, then the next step is to surrender your will absolutely and irrevocably to Jesus. That was not a simple task for me because I have always been one to say, "I got this" and would get it done. The truth is, I do not have this, because after I accepted Christ as Lord and Savior, He had to destroy my arrogant ego, which was above all things important to me. My perception of life was self-motivated in that I believed I could conquer all things placed in my path because my arrogant ego was in charge. The term "Ego" means "Edging God out."

It took some time for Jesus to get it through my thick head that I was riding the horse of self-motivation which is not a completely bad gift to have, however, self-motivation tempered with the will of God directing my pathway to obedience unto Him, brings to light a level of confidence in Christ which allowed me to go forth in His strength, therefore having the confidence of righteous perception in my duty to God. We must not become overconfident which may lead to selfish temptation. So then, how do we overcome the temptation? By staying in the Word of God, it will prepare us for the battles that will come. If we live with Him, we must also die with Him. We are called to be a new creation, ambassadors for Christ, and do it to bring glory to Him by abiding in Him. God will not forget those whom He calls. (Heb. 6:10).

**"Fear thou not; for I *am* with thee: be not dismayed; for I *am* thy God: I will strengthen thee; yea, I will help thee; yea, I will uphold thee with the right hand of my righteousness," (KJV, Isa. 41:10).**

If we desire to do it and follow through with it, then the result is justified. Folks, there are no justifications in the room of indecision; let our yes be yes and our no be no, thus allowing the chips to fall where they may. I must satisfy a desire with an action, be it a righteous or unrighteous action, otherwise, it is mired in the mud of indecision. Saul (Later Paul), had the desire to do the work of God and he perceived it to be his calling. His heart was set on the destruction of Christianity. He had the desire, however, he lacked the blessing from God. Saul failed to understand that God sees our future; therefore, He directs our path to His calling, overriding any self-infused ideas. God has the game plan, but we must open the playbook study the plan, and then seek His will through prayer and obedience to His will, not ours.

Saul of Tarsus (Paul), as did King Saul in the Old Testament, went headstrong ahead in his will, not God's. Now get this: when the Lord got Saul's (Paul's) direction corrected, lives changed, and Christianity exploded across the then-known world. Do not doubt that God can use you. **"Fear thou not; for I am with thee."** Obedience to God requires an action on our behalf.

God acts on our behalf. **"I will strengthen thee; yea, I will help thee.** "Seeking His will requires prayerfully gleaning the wisdom from the pages of His Holy Word (The Playbook) and allowing the Holy Spirit to guide. Think about this; was Saul indwelled with the Holy Spirit as he marched across the land arresting Christians? No. Scripture makes the account that Saul, now Paul, must wait for the laying on of hands by Ananias to receive the Holy Spirit. (Acts 9:10-19).

A human brings the message. A human is a tool or an instrument of God and we must not hinder His helping hand, **"…Yea, I will uphold thee with the right hand of my righteousness,"** meaning to pass by unnoticed. God called Saul "Paul," and prepared him for bringing the Gospel message to the Gentiles. When the fear of Saul the hunter came around; the church scattered, thus helping the church to expand further out from Jerusalem by the spreading of the Gospel Acts 1:8.

God used Saul's mission to destroy the ancient church to expand the church even further into the known world. What Saul failed to realize in his most earnest endeavor in life was not in the will of God. He was a man of great learning dedicated to his mission with a devout devotion to the Law of Moses.

There are many people in our world today who attain great secular learning, and yet fail at recognizing the simple things in life. Unlike modern religion, Christianity does not saddle the believer with great deeds, rules, and or works to gain access to eternal life. Jesus' message of salvation is a simple process of confession of sin, the need for forgiveness, and belief in His death and resurrection, and best of all, the love and grace of our creator.

Romans 10: 9-10 is clear as water, and in John 14:6 Jesus is the only door to eternal life. There is no mention of baptism, no amount of works, or a certain denomination, manmade structure, or any human as a requirement for salvation.

## Personal Study Reflection Notes

### What Have I Learned?

# CHAPTER 3

## THE VISION OF OBEDIENCE

**"And Ananias went his way and entered the house; and laying his hands on him he said, 'Brother Saul, the Lord Jesus who appeared to you on the road as you came, has sent me that you may receive your sight and be filled with the Holy Spirit," (NKJV, Acts 9:17).** (Compare Hos. 6:1-2).

The important factor concerning verse seventeen is the actions of obedience by Ananias. He went to the house as directed by Jesus in a vision. Now watch this. Ananias called him Brother Saul as he laid his hands upon him. (1) The term brother depicts the acceptance by Ananias who had just raised concerns about the stories of Saul of Tarsus and the evil he had committed against the saints, verses 13-14. (2) Jesus explained to Ananias that Saul saw Ananias in a vision from the Lord verse 12. (3) Verse 15. Ananias received the command to go immediately, and he obeyed. (4) Jesus commanded Ananias to go, and nurse Saul back to health, verse 19. Even though Saul committed heinous crimes against the saints. Verse 15 says the Lord has chosen Saul to bring the salvation message to the Gentiles (us), Kings, and the children of Israel. Folks, that is the path to salvation, Amen.

Now, notice here that although Saul committed heinous crimes against the saints, our Lord shall have compassion on him, therefore turning the grief into compassion. If God starts something, He finishes it.?"

**"For I will show him how many things he must suffer for My name's sake," (NKJV, Acts 9:16),** (Compare 2 Cor. 11:24-28).

Verse 16 suggests that Saul, once the hunter of saints, will now become the hunted. The very men he once stood tall among shall desire to kill him, and he will suffer, as did the saints. Actions and deeds do not go unnoticed by God, or by the non-believer. "Words alone are weightless, as actions reveal their true value." Ponder this thought. Many ponder how a loving God can love those who do not believe in his Son, or commit heinous crimes against children and others. Accepting or rejecting Christ at death seals a person's eternal fate. I was 26 years old when God called me to come forward and receive His Son as my Savior. It was a simple answer; were we not all non-believers before salvation? Saul was a non-believer and a murderer before his conversion. He was as we were before our conversion, completely lost.

God chose Saul just as he chose us according to Acts 9:15. Jesus gave us examples of those who took His Word and proclaimed it to the world, making disciples, who will do the same thing, and they are the examples we as modern disciples, are to follow, (Matthew 28:19-20).

Our earnest expectation should be our vision of reaching the lost for Christ, thus allowing Him to work within us. It is impossible to do this alone. Therefore upon our converting to Christ according to Romans 10:9-10, we are then filled with the indwelling of the Holy Spirit thereby allowing the power of God's Word to perform the spiritual duties to which we are called. We are deep in spiritual warfare, and physical human nature alone cannot battle the spiritual evil forces against that which stands against us. The Word of God is our weapon of choice in which there is no defect or defeat. When we dress in the full armor of God, we cannot fail in battle with the Word of God as our weapon of choice. His earnest expectation is for us to be obedient to His calling. Now get this: "Calling and suffering are connected." Why? Four reasons, 1. Because we are image bearers. 2. Because we sin. 3. Because we are being equipped. 4. Because it is ordained. None of the apostles escaped it and likewise, we should expect the same.

Many times, new converts suffer defeat because they lack follow-up training. That is why Scripture says that before new converts enter the battle, they first must drink the milk of simple knowledge before engaging in combat.

The military puts the recruits through the rigors of training before sending them into battle. Experience has taught military leaders that an untrained recruit never comes home. A recruit must learn how to think, act, and train with the tools of warfare before stepping onto the battlefield, even when the odds stand against him or her. The new covert moves from the milk to the solid meat of biblical knowledge before stepping onto the spiritual battlefield of evangelism.

Any task in life requires one to believe in what they are doing. It stems from what they believe to be true. James 2 says, "Having faith without action is an empty faith." actions involve belief. Therefore, how we judge any situation at hand depends on what our eyes and ears send to the brain, which causes our estimation of the situation to fall under our perceived judgment of thought. The Word of God is our training manual, the Holy Spirit is our guide to understanding God's training manual against the Spiritual battles and struggles of this world.

I believe that until we train a new convert to face the rigors of sharing God's Word with the lost, they are open to full-on attack by the deceiver. One who believes they can go about their daily life after conversion and not get involved in the battle to bring the Gospel to the lost is one whom the devil delights. The devil has his army of demons who are on the prowl seeking those who are weak in the faith. Weakness is not always a bad thing when we view weakness in its contextual form.

The Word of God is our training manual, therefore, it becomes the tool of study for our answers to the non-believer's questions or condemnations against us. Even though we are weak, we are not without the power of God to overcome the adversary's attacks, Amen. (Read 2 Kings 6:15-17).

Paul, in his journeys, encountered love, hate, suffering, torture, blessings, a shipwreck, hunger, thirst, eyesight difficulties, joy even prison, disappointments, and many other attributes of life.

Paul used every circumstance to his advantage to further the Gospel of Christ, and yet, he never entertained the idea of giving up the fight. Paul was purpose-driven in his quest to spread the Gospel to the world. Paul was a radical Christian bent on serving the Lord. There is a right way and a wrong way to be radical. Righteous radical, or a deceptive and conniving radical that feeds on fear and destruction. Jesus taught of the peace and the rigors of salvation in Him.

**"These things I have spoken unto you, that in me ye might have peace. In the world ye shall have tribulation: but be of good cheer; I have overcome the world," (KJV, Jn. 16:33),** (Compare 2 Tim. 2:16 concerning unsound doctrine, etc.).

It's when, not if, we encounter tribulation during our service in God's calling. I can assure you that God already knows it and has instilled His plan for our care. Therefore, we are not to be ashamed of our duty to God. Now, watch this, Jesus lays down the truth of coming events in the lives of His disciples, and this includes Saul (Paul), although he has yet to encounter the tribulation coming up in his pre-Damascus life-altering encounter with the Lord. God has called us to a Holy calling not of works but of grace. (2 Cor. 1:9). That calling may include suffering and rejection by the worldly inhabitants of the earth, including family members.

**"For the which cause I also suffer these things: nevertheless I am not ashamed: for I know whom I have believed, and am persuaded**

that he is able to keep that which I have committed unto him against that day," (KJV, 2 Tim. 1:12). (See 1 Cor. 3:12).

Persecution comes from a world filled with hate for the ones who do not conform to its evil ways. A religion based on rules and works is not a genuine belief in Christ, which is by faith. For it is based on conformity to false teachings and the human misunderstanding of contextual truth. Be prepared to face resistance to that truth.

**"The Son of man must suffer many things, and be rejected of the elders and chief priest and scribes, and be slain, and be raised the third day," (KJV, Luke 9:22),** (Compare Lk. 22:37; Jn. 3:14).

Jesus Himself shall suffer many things, which depicts the true value of following Him. I say value because the rewards are greater to come than the present empty desires of our fleshly human nature. Understand that suffering, rejection, and disappointments are in our quest to share the Gospel. Jesus made it clear in His example that we, too, shall experience trials and tribulations because the world hated Him first.

**"And he said to *them* all, If any *man* will come after me, let him deny himself, and take up his cross daily, and follow me," (KJV, Luke 9:23).**

To them, "all" includes us Christians and the Apostle Paul and the disciples. "Any man," meaning any living human must deny him or herself. Folks, there are no exclusions in the verse. We all have a cross to bear, and we must deny our fleshly will daily, for the Gospel trail is laden with hairpin turns, potholes, and slippery slopes.

**"For whosoever will save his life shall lose it: but whosoever will lose his life for my sake, the same shall save it," (KJV, Luke 9:24).**

One writer in his writings says that God has a view of our selfish, fleshly nature, and He writes, "Mine own righteousness." Can we admit it was nothing shy of legal righteousness which God sees as "filthy rags?" Paul viewed his unusual conversion as a "marvelous transformation." What can we say about our conversion, as seen in the eyes of God? Paul gave it all up, including the claim to his misguided righteousness. Like Paul, we cannot receive the grace and righteousness of Christ by faith unless we abandon self-will. There are no alternatives.

A futuristic change occurred in Paul's life after he took hold of the rock of salvation and wrapped his entire worth around it. The Apostle Paul knew the law forward and backward. He breathed the law, he bled the law, and he lived the law. Jesus changed Paul's direction, and suddenly the mysteries of the law became vibrant in his heart and mind. Paul became like a modern freight train on tracks of fiery sparks. His mission in life was now in full-blown motion to spread the Gospel of Christ, and the rest is history. Paul placed his entire fiber into the hands of Jesus.

Paul's second letter to Timothy chapter one exhorts Timothy to stir up the gift of God in him. Paul remembered Timothy verse 3; claiming that young Timothy Chapter possessed an "unfeigned" faith verse 5. The Apostle Paul continues to advise the young Timothy to not "fear "and to relish in the power of love and a sound mind verse 7. Paul then passes on to young Timothy with more exhortation.

**"Be not thou therefore ashamed of the testimony of our Lord, nor of me his prisoner: but be thou partaker of the afflictions of the gospel according to the power of God; Who hath saved us, and called *us* with an holy calling, not according to our works, but according to his own purpose and grace, which was given us in Christ Jesus before the world began," (KJV, 2 Tim. 1:8-9).**

Paul recognized the power of human persuasion in that they may persuade a young convert to feel ashamed of his newfound faith, which is the Gospel of Christ which is outside the confines of Jewish

Law. At first, I was hesitant to share the Gospel due to my lack of understanding. The outside world may use guilt and hate to bring doubt and fear upon a new convert. We witness such behavior in our modern anti-god government and the education system. I felt the devil's attack when I shunned my flesh addiction and converted to Christ. Anti-god leadership and educational systems around the world strive to denounce Jesus Christ as anything but God in human form. Some admit that he was a great prophet but nothing else (Compare Jn. 17:20-21).

We, as believers in Christ, must understand that the lost do not know how lost they truly are. There are but two places for my sin: either upon me or at the cross. Therefore, one must examine his or her heart to discover the truth of sin's location.

Fellowship with God produces a yearning to be in His presence. I believe many Christians, including myself, fall short of an involved fellowship with God. The word ashamed carries tremendous weight in some circumstances in the life of believers. Being ashamed is not just for believers. Words from a nonbeliever are powerful and hurtful to the inexperienced ego of the recently converted believer.

**"Having a good conscience; that, whereas they speak evil of you, as of evildoers, they may be ashamed that falsely accuse your good conversation in Christ," (KJV, 1 Pet. 3:16).**

Some readers might find the King James Version confusing, and I did. I could not get a handle on it. It took suffering for my mind to say, Lord, help to understand. Now, watch this; God can use slanderous actions or suffering by persecutors to lead those lost souls to Christ, verse 17. Whatever the reason behind God's will in our suffering, the Apostle Peter teaches that it is better to suffer for doing good than it is for doing evil. Contrary to the false teaching of the prosperity denominations, the will of God does not always involve wealth, health, and ease of life. Now, watch this; it may very well involve or even require hardship and abuse, therefore prompting the age-old question of, "Why would God ever want that to happen?" This is a question that continues to bring doubt, (a tool of Satan) into the debate. God never promised sinful-natured humanity a road of roses. Though the rose blossoms, there will be thorns to navigate on that road.

1 Peter chapter 2:6 depicts Christ as the chief corner-stone. He is our foundation, the anchor to which we can cling to. He is the one who suffered enormously for our sake. Verse 18 depicts the duty of the servants. Verse 21 anchors the truth of Christ as our example. Therefore, it is not surprising to learn that we, as servants of our God, our creator, may be called to suffer the same for His sake. The Apostle Paul lived on that rocky road his entire ministry, even unto death. I do not believe Paul had any reason to be ashamed of preaching the Gospel. The word "ashamed" is not just a New Testament term.

**"Then there went *certain*, and told David how the men were served, And he sent to meet them: for the men were greatly ashamed. And the king said, Tarry at Jericho until your beards be grown, and *then* return," (KJV, 1 Chron. 19:5).**

This is a story about how some of King David's men were treated by Hanun, Chapter 19:1-4. The gesture made by David was in kindness. However, the princes of the children of Ammon twisted David's kindness into evil. A good Bible study on the term "shamed or ashamed" will cover 111 verses from 30 books starting with Genesis 2:25.

King David was no stranger to heartache, suffering, and controversy brought on by his sin. Biblical history proves that the children of God will suffer for His purpose, Amen.

If we consider the historical facts of the Jewish people, we will learn of the disastrous roads on which they traveled. Not the roads of terrible terrain, but the roads of misguided prayers and actions. Does that twist your mind somewhat? History shows that the Jewish people, much like many Christians today, often try to persuade God's direction in their lives to satisfy their selfish desires, including wealth gain.

Let us look at Habakkuk as an example. The question that arises is why God delays doing anything about particular situations. Habakkuk cannot understand why God would permit His people to be enslaved by a wicked nation. Habakkuk questions God on this matter. Do we not do the same thing? Do we not ask why? There is a temptation in man's selfishness to use prayer to control or direct God's direction in His plans for humanity. Now watch this. The response Habakkuk received conclusively affirms that God is not accountable to any person and is not obligated to comply with human ideas or demands of how He should handle any situation. He is completely wise and sovereign in all His dealings with humanity. Some may disagree and yet, for others, it may come as a complete surprise. Yes, God hears and answers our prayers; however, He does not answer the selfish misaligned prayers of an egotistical saint or unsaved sinner. God is not a vending machine of earthly desires.

God has set His plan for humanity's present and future in stone, and we can find guidance in the Book of Revelation.

We cannot attempt to sway God's direction. Scripture makes clear God uses evil people to wake us up to fully trust in Him. Are we not living under the same unrighteous indignation of godless leadership? (Prov. 38:2-26) The Jews lived under Saul. God allowed the Jews their heart's desire for a king because they did not like being under the judgment of God's judge; they wanted to be like other nations and their hearts' desires backfired on them. How do we define such actions?

**1.** Righteous. An action; characterized by justice or uprightness; morally right or justifiable.

**2.** Indignation. Anger at what is unworthy or wrongful; wrath excited by a sense of wrong, or by meanness, injustice, wickedness, or misconduct; righteous or dignified anger.

**3**. God has righteous indignation–holy anger, fury, and jealousy at sinners (Psa. 69:24; 78:49; Isa. 30:27,-30; Jer. 10:10; Ezek. 21:31; 22:31; Nahum 1:6; Mal. 1:4; Micah. 7:9; Hab. 3:12; Zep. 3:8; Zech 1:12).

Human nature is the direct opposition to the will and nature of God. After the fall in the Garden of Eden, humanity suffered a tremendous loss of blessings that God had planned for His creation to enjoy.

Some may ask why God allowed Satan to intervene. God's love is not based on rules and regulations enforced by taskmasters. His love is based on His character or His nature to love. I do not believe humanity will fully understand the true loving nature of God on this side of Heaven. I believe it is one of the many aspects of God that awaits those (believers) who have not yet passed into the eternal state. Those who have passed now understand the tremendous rewards of life without pain and suffering. Amen.

# CHAPTER 4

## THE POWER OF GOD UNTO SALVATION

"For I am not ashamed of the gospel of Christ: for it is the power of God unto salvation to every one that believeth; to the Jew first, and also to the Greek. For therein is the righteousness of God revealed from faith to faith: as it is written, The just shall live by faith," (KJV, Rom. 1:16-17).

Our faith reveals our calling from God. God's Holy Word reveals to the believer what the world cannot understand. His Word is illogical even to the highest level of educated humanity. Without the empowerment of the Holy Spirit, great minds cannot grasp the simple concept of God's power unto salvation.

A new convert to Christ called by God eliminates the secret door of salvation, thus placing him or herself on a remarkable path of understanding life that the great minds without God cannot comprehend. The Bible depicts Moses as a man of meekness (Num. 12:3), yet, in our minds, we may not think of him in such a way. Moses rose in great wealth and privileges, and as an Egyptian Prince, he possessed all the great learning Egypt offered, and yet, his Hebrew birth mother, a godly woman, instilled within him the teachings of God. This is where the conflict began-God against pagan false gods. Moses' mother, Jochebed, passed on to Moses her great faith and trust in God. Moses refused to continue the wealth and fame and returned to his parent's lifestyle of slavery. The power of God's salvation reflects the very beginning of humanity. Listen to King David as he pours out his heart to God.

"I have preached righteousness in the great congregation: lo, I have not refrained my lips, O Lord though knowest. I have not hid thy righteousness within my heart; I have declared thy faithfulness

**and thy salvation: I have not concealed thy truth from the great congregation," (KJV, Psa. 40:9-10).**

David reflects on the concept of not being ashamed as he addresses the Lord in verse 9. He states he has proclaimed God's works to the great congregation, meaning unto all the faithful people of Israel as did Paul after his conversion. King David held nothing back when he reported how the Lord rescued him from his enemies and the Apostle Paul reflects the power of God's mercy through all his trials and sufferings in which he proclaimed it all to Christ. God purposed His divine attributes, such as trustworthiness and love, toward all of His people, and that includes us.

Be not ashamed to bring all things to God. When God calls us to serve, we do not define the conditions. As servants, we are to give back to Him (God) what He deserves. Our Father in Heaven will honor those who serve Him. We are to do our work as unto the Lord. Ponder this truth: We are servants of God, not servants of the church. Now, watch this. If God is our boss, then it is He who determines our reward. Our motivation for excellent work should be as working for God, amen.

The Apostle Paul and the disciples of Christ lived unto death with the concept of excellent work. Was it not viewed as working for the Kingdom of God? Never did they feel their labor and deeds granted them direct access to Heaven, as do some in our modern post-ascension of Christ religions. Some believe that, alongside faith, we must work our way to Heaven. If that were the case, the cross was a sham and Jesus died for our deeds of labor and not for the forgiveness of our sins.

Cowering away to the side of the conflict of disagreement of who Christ is and why He suffered the cross is nothing less than being ashamed of what one truly believes in their heart. We are to speak boldly with affection and comfort in our desire to serve God and be joyful, even in affliction.

However, we must not cross the line by becoming arrogant tools of the devil. What does arrogant mean?

"Ar-ro-gant" is an adjective of Middle English (arrogant-arrogans) "presuming." Making claims or pretensions to superior importance or overbearing, assuming insolently proud. An attitude of superiority manifested in an overbearing manner or presumptuous claims or assumptions.

We live in a secular world, therefore arrogance and leadership go hand-in-hand. Now, watch this. Cocky and confident are adjectives that describe a seemingly successful leader. Here is the kicker that should hit us square in the heart. Most churches, according to one survey, claim that church members want a humble pastor; yet in reality, churches and Christian ministries have positioned themselves to attract and create arrogant leaders because ministry is largely results-driven, just as secular society is self-idolized and motivated.

Does this description of being a confident leader not cause a stir within your soul? Our modern churches seem to want popular, hip, self-assured go-getters to fill the pulpit. However, we might be unintentionally leaning toward proud leaders, therefore breeding arrogant and proud mentors who one day may fall from their self-made pedestals, meaning the same pedestals we may have put them upon.

**"Pride *goes* before destruction, And a haughty spirit before a fall. Better *to be* of a humble spirit with the lowly, Than to divide the spoil with the proud," (NKJV, Prov. 16:18-19).**

One may ask what this has to do with the Power of God unto salvation. The simple truth is these types of church leaders are plentiful on national and social media. The most obvious sign is bragging about their accomplishments and the influential people they hang with, dwelling on self-promotion.

**"They utter speech, *and* speak insolent things; All the workers of iniquity boast in themselves," (NKJV, Psa. 94:4).**

A recent survey result claimed that arrogant leaders love attention. They can be introverts or extroverts. Look folks, regardless of personality, it is human nature to love attention because it makes us feel better. There is much more to this survey. However, the focus is that prideful arrogance in any leader or leadership opens the door to false teaching or creating doubt which begins as a crack, and the devil will use it to widen the opening and possibly taint the base of our faith in Christ Jesus. Preaching righteousness and sound doctrinal teaching from the pulpit and classroom creates the barrier that guards against the cancer of false teachings that plague our world today. An old hymn says:

"At even ere the sun was set," and, there is the line, "No word from Him can fruitless fall." The simple truth of what type of leadership a body may have is if they are not placing Christ in the center of all things, meaning above all things, including themselves, they are not in obedience to God. Amen.

Take hold of this truth: "Our salvation is anchored in God's mercy and grace and not to any fruitless merit from our selfish indulgence. We cannot in ourselves merit any foundational reason to expect our works to provide the salvation that belongs to the author of salvation alone. His work shall not be hindered when Christ is in the center of all things."

One writer had this to say, "We can apply the prophecy of Isaiah, which can be applied to the matchless and eternal words, leaving the holy lips of Jesus when he walked among men."

**"So shall my word be that goeth forth out of my mouth; it shall not return unto me void, but it shall accomplish that which I please, and it shall prosper** *in the thing* **whereto I sent it," (KJV, Isa. 55:11).**

It is the divine nature of Jesus Christ in which the divine source and substance of His teachings can never fail. "The word which ye hear is not mine," he could say, **"But the Father's which sent me,"** (references to John 14:24). Therefore, it is the secret of the abiding influence of His divine utterances, and only eternity alone will reveal the marvelous results of all that Jesus taught, therefore, we have available to us the immediate effects of His teachings along with the continuing influence of His grace, (see Psa. 45:2).

The one who does not love Christ in a radical and personal manner will not love the Body, nor will they have a love for the lost to come to Christ. The unsaved members of humanity perceive modern celebrity preachers as self-motivated toward wealth and fame. Folks, it is not our job to judge them, or publicly condemn them, (See Matthew 6:5).

Early in my Christian conversion, I learned that a pastor who truly loves the Lord and willingly seeks to evangelize in the wilderness of lost souls beyond the steps of the physical building is a pastor whom God has called, even unto suffering for the sake of Christ. He willingly abandons worldly ways for the sake of Christ to ensure that salvation by faith in Christ for all humanity remains the top priority. Listen, I am not judging anyone, however, I have sat under the teachings of flashy motivated pastors and quickly grown tired of the self-indulgence coming from the pulpit. What percentage of the message is about the love of Christ for the lost souls compared to the amount spent on the gifts of the Holy Spirit, the building or a mega-church building, or personal wealth?

Jesus was never flashy; therefore, the lost saw the heart of Christ and not the wealth which whitewashes the truth with a gray tint. Many bodies of Christ have fallen victim to worldly influences in that being flashy sells air time and fills the coffer. Jesus was never flashy, nor were the Apostles. While many believers may see a flashy dress, jewelry, mega buildings, and worldly possessions as successful or maybe even blessed, a realist non-believer sees it as a con. We must think about the purpose of our witness to the lost souls within the oceans of humanity. What are the flashy ministries promoting? Is it Jesus and eternal salvation, or is it wealth and fame? God knows and He will deal with it in His time, not ours. Remember, we are not to be the judge of another's heart. We are not to leave the door of temptation open enough for the deceiver to slip in a wedge for a later opportunity to expand the opening, Amen.

Jesus never promoted earthly wealth as a reason for salvation. When we allow the cross to become the step ladder to wealth and fame, we are exercising the will of the devil and not the will of God. AMEN.

Jesus desires that we become fishers of men for the Gospel and not the earthly gold coin of success and wealth. Our mission on Earth as Disciples of Christ is the same as God's purpose for sending His Son to reconcile His creation back unto Him.

The power of God unto salvation does not and cannot come from the human perspective of self-motivation. Our motivation and mission as true Christians to evangelize the oceans of lost souls must come from the source of our salvation, Jesus Christ. It was the purpose of God Himself to hang on the cross as the sacrificial lamb of forgiveness for the sins of humanity. Without His sacrifice, we stand condemned to hell.

# Personal Study Reflection Notes

## What Have I Learned?

# CHAPTER 5

## FAITH CREATES CHANGE

Change is based on faith in Christ, not self-will, power, position, or intelligence. Jesus reveals in His teaching what only God could reveal to the seeker. The essence of the God-to-man dialogue is about change, the change necessary to enter the Kingdom of God. Faith is the pathway to change. It changes us, and the change wrought in us by faith is the transition from spiritual death to spiritual life.

A certain man of the Pharisees named Nicodemus, a man of great power and influence, visited Jesus under the cover of night to inquire about Jesus' purpose for His arrival in Jerusalem, which caused great concern among the ruling heads of the Jews.

**"There was a man of the Pharisees name Nicodemus, a ruler of the Jews: The same came to Jesus by night, and said unto him, Rabbi, we know that thou art a teacher come from God: for no man can do these miracles that thou doest, except God be with him," (KJV, Jn. 3:1-2).**

The Jews believed in God and the law to the very core of their being. From what they wrote about the Jews, we find faith is not at the top of their priority list. Their faith rested in the Law of Moses, which they adhered to even unto death, and demanded the same from the nation. The Jews were already in turmoil over John the Baptist (Matthew Chapter 3).

Now another man comes along preaching repentance. (Matt. 5:17) and performing miracles and making converts. Jesus' teaching confounded the Jewish leadership, their minds spinning in circles because great multitudes followed Him. (Matt. 5:25).

The Gospel of Matthew is about fulfillment. Some say he specifically presents Jesus as the new Moses in that he does so by presenting Jesus as the teacher of Israel through five discourses that mirror the ways presented in the Pentateuch in which Jesus presented during the sermon on the mount. Now, he never calls Jesus the new Moses. However, the imagery presented is unblemished in that Jesus is the new prophet who establishes the new covenant not with the animal blood sacrifice, but of His blood poured out for the sins of humanity. Therefore, not by works, but by grace through faith are we saved.

Faith can be a powerful ally under adverse conditions and the Jewish masses were not as strong in their faith in God as they were in the religious law of Moses. The Jewish nation was under siege by the Roman Empire and the Jewish leadership wanted the Romans gone. I do not believe it is too farfetched to believe Nicodemus not only came under the cover of night but also a mask of deception of his purpose. However, I believe Nicodemus was a man seeking a deeper understanding of God in that deep within, beat the heart of a godly man. Many believe he sought wisdom and an ally with this teacher to help overthrow the Roman government. The Jews were looking for the Messiah; however, they expected him to show up with a mighty army and overthrow the Romans.

The prophets of old wrote of the Messiah's coming; however, over time, the Jewish leadership not only added to the details but also misinterpreted the timing and the details of how He shall come. The calling of God is a mystery even to some believers who claim Christ as the savior. Should we not look to Christ and His Word for all the answers concerning life's mysteries? As believers, our earnest expectations dare not be of worldly riches and notoriety, but centered on Christ, our sacrificial lamb, and how our duty to Him brings a boatload of emotions and missteps. Above all, we are to rejoice, as did Paul in all things, because God did not promise us a road covered with roses in this life to travel.

Having affection for Christ is to be an overcomer, and our belief requires action in all things. Some may say I am not strong enough to overcome anything. Want to know a simple truth? Strength does not come from what we can do. Strength comes from overcoming the things we once believed we couldn't do. One thing I learned the hard way was I needed to step out of my comfort zone so that Christ could make my devotion to Him stronger and allow me to grow. I think that courage and strength are not separate. When we allow ourselves to feel ashamed either by failed attempts at something or we are being shamed for our belief. Are we not opening the door to doubt and confusion when we yield ourselves to someone or something other than Jesus Christ?

Our ultra-modern cultural world has become a work to survive sewer pits of selfish indulgence. It lacks spiritual direction. Therefore, what's missing in our culture today? What do I earnestly expect out of this temporary life on planet Earth?

Many, including myself, need help answering such questions because circumstances may change daily. Let us be honest; many are hurting and confused about life and are tired of living on the ragged edge of day-to-day existence.

Modern culture promotes the idea that God made a mistake in His gender design, meaning a person may not be comfortable living as a male or female and desires to change God's design. That is nothing short of saying, "God, you made a mistake in me, and I am going to change it."

The above example is the most focused on anti-god design in our temporary human existence today. Living on the ragged edge covers a boatload of addictions and emotional confusion that comes from one source the devil and is for his deceptive and destructive purpose.

King David's response to God's grace provides for those who truly love God a worthy model for us all to imitate, just as Paul lived his faith in Christ and left us another example to follow.

David shows us that those who truly love the Lord are those who have properly responded to His love for them and are living in faith unto Him. By reflecting on David's Psalms, we find at least three important observations.

**1.** We who truly love God have experienced His power to deliver us from circumstances. Therefore our fears are gone.

**2.** We who truly love God have received His peace and forgiveness, meaning our guilt has been relieved.

**3.** Feeling God's presence through affliction and truly loving Him has strengthened our faith.

Many believe afflictions strengthened the Apostle Paul's faith and continued to spread the Gospel. Even though the possibility of death followed behind every step he took, his faith in Christ lighted his path. That strong faith is available to all Christians, as it was to the apostles. How can we define our most earnest expectations as Christians if our faith in Jesus is like a rudderless ship in stormy seas? The waves of life will toss us about and carry us far away, deeper into an endless sea of despair. One writer put it this way: "Sorrow looks back; worry looks around; but faith looks up."

Hannah's yoke of sorrow weighed her down. The word "Anak," in Hebrew means chain or neck chain. A chain around the neck is this picture of a yoke that weighs a person down. She came to the end of herself and prayed to God for a son. Hannah was on a dead-end road in her life. She had to either abandon her wish to have a son or opt for the lone alternative. I am sure we all have come to a dead-end of sorts in our quest for something positive in our lives. One writer said, "She took on the throne attitude of Jesus."

The same writer also said, "Having a throne attitude" means we ought to know our place in Christ. Jesus trusted all things to the Father in Heaven. It is an attitude of resting in God who makes our enemies our footstools." We are to have a winning attitude mentality. Stopping the struggling allows God to take control of the rudder, keeping the ship on course. Was he correct? I lean toward the yes answer.

It does not matter how strong you might think you are in the Lord. Christians constantly feel the weight of guilt; it is because many Christians do not understand the difference between conviction and guilt. We are mere humans, and emotional turmoil is sitting on our doorstep. Our strength is in our faith in Christ, and our hope knows that our eternal destination is Heaven. Conviction comes from God when sin has separated our connection with Him. If our focus and earnest concerns are the woes of this temporary existence in the flesh, dare we say that is where our hope lies? God is a God of love, and He wants us to be 100% free from sin.

Guilt comes from Satan, and he will constantly accuse and harass us by reminding us of our past, meaning sins from which we have already repented. We do not stand guilty of those sins after repenting. Satan has a bag of guilt to place upon us for our past sins and will bring them up every time.

Are you washed in the soul-cleansing blood of the Lamb? Are your garments spotless? Are they white as snow?

**"Let us draw near with a true heart in full assurance of faith, having our hearts sprinkled from an evil conscience, and our bodies washed with pure water," (KJV, Heb. 10:22).**

Has your faith in Christ brought a change in your lifestyle, your mind, your heart, and your prayer life?

*"Oh! Precious is the flow that makes me white as snow; No other fount I know, nothing but the blood of Jesus."*

**"Blessed *is he whose* transgressions *is* forgiven, *Whose* sin is covered. Blessed is the man to whom the Lord does not impute iniquity, and in whose spirit *there is* no guile," (KJV, Psa. 32:1-2).**

God took the blunt force of humanity's sin and placed it squarely on the shoulders of His Son, Jesus. We who are in Christ bear no weight of condemnation. Jesus suffered to set us free, amen.

**"Who being the brightness of *his* glory, and the express image of his person, and upholding all things by the word of his power, when he had by himself purged our sins, sat down on the right hand of the Majesty on high," (KJV, Heb. 1:3).**

Hebrews 1:3 reminds us of the Trinity. It depicts the sound doctrinal teaching that Jesus is 100 % God and 100% man. It also reveals to us the different nature of God.

Throughout the Scripture, we see the one true God the Father, God the Son, and God the Holy Spirit as the Trinitarian God.

Jesus Christ can be no one else but God, creator of the universe and all things therein.

### PERSONAL THOUGHTS
### WHAT HAVE I LEARNED

# CHAPTER 6

## YIELDING TO CHRIST

Here is a good saying, "Actions always reveal why only words cannot hold any weight."

**"Therefore, to him who knows to do good and does not do *it*, to him it is sin," (NKJV, James 4:17), (Compare Luke 12:47).**

James backs the above by saying, "Actions speak louder than words." Knowledge is good to have to a point. However, a head full of knowledge is useless unless we set the knowledge in motion to act. Words without deeds are meaningless. A song is not a song without words. Loving others without action is a weak concept of caring for another.

**"But the wisdom that is from above is first pure, then peaceable, gentle, willing to yield, full of mercy and good fruits, without partially and without hypocrisy. Now the fruit of righteousness is sown in peace by those who make peace," (NKJV, James 3:17-18).**

Above all else, what is the first aspect of decision-making? Wisdom from above; from wisdom flows all else. The following points helped me to place my decision-making process into a perspective that made more sense. I need to remember not to:

**1.** To give way to pressure or influence, submitting or submitting to urging, persuasion, or entreaty.

**2.** To give up and cease resistance, contention, submission, or succumbing to facing an enemy who would not yield or yield to temptation.

How does one yield all to God? The following six points will ease the confusion, starting with prayer.

**1.** Complete prayer; is the first step to surrender.

**2.** Change our perspective.

**3.** Having a direct line to God comes through prayer.

**4.** Shift our focus to our creator.

**5.** Place our plans before Him as we seek direction.

**6.** Prayer reminds us to seek His will.

The knowledge of God is spiritual and is not carnal (earthly thinking), so to yield to Jesus is to avoid our earthly desires and thinking.

The first ten words of verse 17, "But the wisdom that is from above is first pure," lays the foundation of what our thought pattern rests on. True wisdom is from above and above all else, it is pure. The result, therefore, is that all things in between produce the righteousness that is sown in peace by those who make peace rather than turmoil.

**"My brethren, do not hold the faith of our Lord Jesus Christ, *the Lord* of glory, with partially," (NKJV, James 2:1).**

Many of the brethren in James' time were excluding the downtrodden and placing the well-to-do above them. James chapter two cautions the brethren to avoid such actions in that doing so you make yourself an evil-thinking judge over others verse 4. God has promised that all who earnestly seek Him in love will enter the Kingdom of God verse 5. Therefore, as in James 4:17, their actions partially are a sin because, as brethren, they know to do good and they chose not to do good by excluding some from the best seats in the house.

Constructed as a physical shelter from the elements, the church building is where everyone is welcome. The physical structure cannot provide salvation. The contents of the message preached within ought to lead all people to the cross of salvation. A church that gives importance to attendance, adornment, and financial status is heading toward destruction. If God does not play the partiality game, then how can the pompous occupants within play God? If we are looking at how people have dressed, our focus is not on the salvation message for the lost. It is on our selfish ego as one who wants to play god and judge.

Yielding to God our entire will includes our desire to be the judge of others. Truly saved individuals were once spiritually downtrodden, and the blessings of the Lord transformed them on the inside and outside. Some take longer than others, so those who sit home and pass judgment on others are nothing short of self-righteous indulged prigs of division, so get over it already and stop playing God because you are the ones who will lose out on the blessings.

Jesus told the prostitute thrown at His feet to stop sinning. He did not condemn her, and He did not say to her, go change your clothes and dress as others. Remove the plank from your eye before trying to remove the sliver from another.

# CHAPTER 7

## YIELDING TO GOD'S PURPOSE

One may ponder God's purpose for their life after their life-altering experience of salvation. So how does one find the answer to such questions?

The most asked questions I believe are the ones I ask myself and fall back on when confronted with a confusing or painful situation.

"What is God's purpose for this in my life?"

"How can I trust what God is up to in my life?"

I will be honest with you. Life throws curve balls, and it will shake our foundation, even our faith. It can be scary. However, rest in the peace of knowing we are not alone in the sea of turmoil and confusion. Experiences in my life have put me on death's doorstep. At least my wife believed it to be so.

It is my belief God uses these circumstances to draw us closer to Him. Our stormy seas rise because of the strong winds of our self-motivated actions. Yes, God may stir the water some when we become overconfident or when we surrender to our comfort zone by buckling up for the long haul.

God's mysterious ways have confounded even the most ardent believer. I am sure that a somewhat weaker knowledgeable individual is confident that they are in good company. God wants us to know that He has not abandoned us and He knows everything about us. He is perfect; He is eternal, and He is Almighty, amen.

**"O Lord, you have searched me and know *me*. You know my sitting down and my rising up; You understand my thought afar off. You comprehend my path and my lying down, And are acquainted with**

all my ways. For *there is* not a word on my tongue, *But behold*, O Lord, You know it altogether," (KJV, Psa. 139:1-4).

However, the truth looms above our heads; we are imperfect and sinful, and our lives are but a vapor (James 4:14). By experience, I have learned that the more I learn, the more I realize how much I don't know.

Ponder this thought. Why in the world wouldn't I align my thoughts with God's purpose? I am not ashamed to admit that I wonder about it. And I am 70. And I believe I learned enough to make my way. I find it best to get over that tendency. I belong to Him and He provides my needs and besides; HE IS GOD, amen.

**"Fear not, for *I am* with you; Be not dismayed, for I *am* your God. I will strengthen you, I will uphold you with My righteous right hand," (NKJV, Isa. 41:10).**

This is God's assurance to His people, and it was not inclusive to just Jews. He handed it down to our post-ascension modern world. We are His people, folks. Some believe God's purpose for an individual is mysterious and hidden. I do not cling to such a belief. Now watch this;

**"With what shall I come before the Lord, *And bow* myself before the High God? Shall I come before Him with burnt offerings, With calves a year old? Will the Lord be pleased with thousands of rams, Ten thousand rivers of oil? Shall I give my firstborn *for* my transgression, The fruit of my body *for* the sin of my soul? He has shown you O man, what is good; And what does the Lord require of you But to do justly, To love mercy, And to walk humbly with your God," (NKJV, Micah 6: 6-8).**

Think about the words of Jesus and how these verses line up with His teaching. Jesus reiterated the foundation of God's will in these verses. What is that saying to us today? It means that we are to lay a foundation for all our actions and make them purposeful, in that we bind our obedience to God to how that purpose is lived out daily. Each day brings new challenges. Therefore, we must adjust our purpose for that day to adhere to the will of God. Amen.

There is no mystery in knowing God's purpose in your life when His Word is clear as spring waters. His absolute loving ways are not lacking in substance; however, many people in our modern world are becoming overwhelmed by the political evil being pushed upon us. The attention span of many today seems short-lived in every aspect of life. We release thoughts into the blowing wind and become distracted because we search and search for that thought's purpose for invading our mind in the first place.

Many times God has called me to certain duties and I get all excited then poof, what was I supposed to do? I attribute that to a lack of motivation to continue. Admitting I lack motivation is more difficult than going through with the plan.

A recent study involving the search for biblical characters that disobeyed God's calling opened my eyes to my selfishness. There are many examples to draw from, (Jer. 7:13-15; Psa. 57:2-3 are but a couple).

Jesus spoke of not doing His will but the will of the Father alone.

**"I can of Myself do nothing As I hear, I Judge; and My judgment is righteous, because I do not seek My own will but the will of the Father who sent Me," (NKJV, Jn. 5:30).**

James 3:17 says that we are to follow Jesus' example because it is the fruit of wisdom a person attains when they are "willing to yield to God's purpose for their life." There is no mystery; there is no secret formula to drink. Yielding to God's purpose acts on our behalf, therefore becoming a workman approved by God. That being said, then what is our responsibility as Christians? Present yourselves as being approved by God as in a workman who does not need to be ashamed and who correctly handles the Word of truth entrusted to him by the creator of the universe.

Love is a positive action; motivation is a byproduct of love as mercy was the byproduct of God's love and grace when Jesus willingly went to the cross that we might attain forgiveness for our sins and be raised on the third day that we may attain eternal life, a choice only we can make as an individual.

When allowing our bodies to be used for something we are yielding to Christ, it may occur more often than not for the unbeliever, and believers, depending on the situation. Christians are not above sinful temptations. Although it is not a sin to be tempted, it is a sin when one decides by action to partake of it. The Lord wants us to yield all to Him, to present our bodies to Him.

**"Neither yield ye your members as instruments of unrighteousness unto sin: but yield yourselves unto God, as those that are alive from the dead, and your members *as* instruments of righteousness unto God," (KJV, Rom. 6:13).**

It becomes our choice to either yield or not. However, we must accept the consequences of our choice because only we alone make the choice. Life's choices belong to the individual alone; we cannot lay the blame on anyone else but ourselves.

If we can yield to God fully (meaning all or none) in life, then we will enjoy life to the fullest, even overflowing. Upon receiving Christ as Lord and Savior (Born Again), God submersed our spirit like Him through Christ Jesus. Ponder this question; why do we not experience an outward life that is even relative to the life such as Christ lived?

Why is it challenging for converts to Christianity to find it difficult to distinguish between our external experiences and daily life? Is the difference on full display, or is it in reserve for when called upon meaning on an as-needed basis? Here is the Biblical truth: When the Holy Spirit has indwelled the believer (after accepting Christ as Savior), there must be a change that is noticed by all.

Let us dig into the answer by reflecting on three simple words: "Yield to God." It doesn't seem complicated. These three simple words that mean by yielding unto Him, He moves in and dwells within us. Now watch this; the degree to the amount of what a person yields willingly, unto Him will determine the amount of Him that is revealed and experienced outwardly daily in us.

Romans 6:13 means we are not to offer our bodies to lustful flesh or an instrument of sinful wickedness. The idea the writer shows is that lustful desires are in the actions of the flesh or the mind. It is still a sin. Fornication in the head is still fornication in the bed. If you think about it, you committed it even without physical contact. Desiring worldly anything results in empty and temporal satisfaction. Yielding that desire to God relieves us of that burden. Therefore, He satisfies the soul in a righteous satisfaction, full and overflowing joy. When we apply God's Word to our lives, it means we are yielding to God that which He desires of us. We are not to use our mouths, minds, hands, eyes, or any member of our body to yield to sin, but to God. Above all, when under temptation's desire we are to pray for deliverance and yield it to God.

The temptation to sin is a full-time resident at the doorstep of depression, pain, discouragement, loss, anger, and hurting hearts. Even in joyful celebration, the temptation of sin is ready to jump in and party hardy. "Come on, man, enjoy this. You only live once; party on, man." A good friend may discourage us from over-indulging; however, a not-so-good friend will always suggest jumping into the whole of the sin. Don't worry, for tomorrow we die.

**"What shall we say then? Shall we continue in sin, that grace may abound? God forbid. How shall we that are dead to sin, live any longer therein? Know ye not, that so many of us as were baptized into Jesus Christ were baptized into His death? Therefore we are buried with him by baptism into death: that like as Christ was raised up from the dead by the glory of the Father, even so we also should walk in newness of life," (KJV, Rom. 6:1-4).**

Therefore, that which shields us from the temptation of sin is that which we may lack in our Christian journey. Should not our earnest expectations center on the one whose mercy reigns? And which He provided us the escape from spiritual death through His only begotten Son?

**"There *is* therefore now no condemnation to them which are in Christ Jesus, who walk not after the flesh, but after the Spirit. For the law of the Spirit of life in Christ Jesus hath made me free from the law of sin and death," (KJV, Rom. 8:1-2).**

There is a part of humanity that believes we can forgive and yet pray to the Lord to forgive that sin, allowing the sinner to repeat the sin again and again. The 21 words in verse 1 blow that belief out the window. Paul never leans in that direction, not even by accident. Go to the little booth and the priest will forgive you your sin. It is not his place to forgive sin; it is the Lord's place, and He paid that price on the cross. Therefore, we possess a direct connection with the Lord; we do not require a human to communicate with us. Jesus Christ is our intercessor. Amen. It is our place to bow before Christ and plead our case for forgiveness. Christ shed His blood for the sins of humanity, but that requires action on our part.

"I say then: Walk in the Spirit, and you shall not fulfill the lust of the flesh. For the flesh lusts against the Spirit, and the Spirit against the flesh; and these are contrary to one another; so that you do not do the things that you wish," (NKJV, Gal. 5:16-17).

Paul affirms that the Holy Spirit and the lust of the flesh were a battle against each other. They cannot co-exist without a conflict. A believer must choose to fulfill the lust of the flesh or allow the Holy Spirit to guide our path away from lustful sin. The lust of the flesh covers many aspects of our earthly travels. The devil is not above pushing the vilest sources of depravity in front of our eyes. Now, watch this.

"Now the works of the flesh are evident, which are: adultery, fornication, uncleanness, lewdness idolatry, sorcery, hatred, contentions, jealousies, outburst of wrath, selfish ambitions, dissensions, heresies, envy, murders, drunkenness, revelries, and the like; of which I tell you beforehand, just as I also told *you* in time past, that those who practice such things will not inherit the kingdom of God," (NKJV, Gal. 5:19-21).

Under the intense pressure of modern media to follow the heathen's concept of true happiness in life, even the hearts of believers may become calloused toward God's pure wisdom, even though, we may know in our hearts that God's Word holds the key to the true knowledge of all things.

"For we wrestle not against flesh and blood, but against principalities, against powers, against the rulers of the darkness of this world, against spiritual wickedness in high *places.* Wherefore take unto you the whole armour of God, that ye may be able to withstand in the evil day, and having done all, to stand," (KJV, Eph. 6:12-13).

Paul speaks to the parents of children, the servant, and his master in chapter six of Ephesians. One may wonder why he addresses the parents. It is because the children are not living in the public education system, although in many cultures they may do so, therefore, the teaching of one's culture and foundation of belief commences in the home at a young age. A significant shift in the government's thinking about who controls a child's education is occurring in our nation. Both major political parties have accepted this change. Parents will lose their right to govern their children in what they learn in public education.

In the last days people will be lovers of themselves, lovers of money, boastful, proud, abusive, disobedient to their parents, ungrateful, unholy, without love, unforgiving, slanderous, blasphemers, without self-control, brutal, not lovers of the good, treacherous, rash, conceited, lovers of pleasure rather than godliness but denying its power. (see 2 Tim. 3: 2-5).

Listen, parents, to what your children are saying, eating, watching on all the media outlets, etc. Ask yourself this simple question, "Will my child or grandchild learn and live a godly type of life, and love others, or will they live as everything listed above?

Take a hard look at what your children are learning from you and/or the worldly media.

Parents today are at war with the public educators who are pushing gender identity. Males that identify as females using female dressing facilities are unnatural. Folks, with all sincerity, should not parents know what the public education system teaches? What should parents expect of their local education system?

**PERSONAL THOUGHTS**

**WHAT HAVE I LEARNED**

# CHAPTER 8

## YIELDING TO THE CALL OF GOD

For the believer, there is but one Christ in which the Christian has but one hope for eternity in Heaven. Therefore, that hope is not singular but inclusive of all believers as a heart of oneness. The translation from the ancient text means a divine calling by which they introduced Christians to the privileges of the Gospel, and they translated the word as "calling."

**"For the gifts and calling of God *are* without repentance," (KJV, Rom. 11:29).**

The gifts and the calling are irrevocable; God does not take back His gifts. He does not change His mind. Jesus said, "My meat is to do the will of him that sent me, and to finish his work," (KJV, Jn. 4:34). Jesus' food was to give eternal life. That was His source of strength; Jesus yielded to the calling of God and all that His Father purposed for Him to do while in the flesh.

**"For I know the thoughts that I think toward you, saith the LORD, thoughts of peace, and not of evil, to give you an expected end," (KJV, Jer. 29:11).**

This is not a promise that immediately rescues us from the hardships or the sufferings experienced in the flesh. Rather, it is a promise that God provides for our lives regardless of our current situation. God deals with each situation because each is different. We are to have confidence that He can work through it to prosper us and provide us with the hope of something better to come.

Yielding and believing in what God can do is inclusive of one another. They cannot be separated. They are both actions that we must act upon if we are to understand the full scope of His plan for our lives here on Earth. I do not pretend to say the task is easy for any believer. Life can be difficult; however, we have hope in Christ to anchor us to Him in the storms of life.

Jesus commissioned His disciples for a future purpose, which He chose them to accomplish. The disciples' minds were on the restoration of Israel, however, it paled miserably when compared to the power that His disciples were about to receive.

The attempt to uncover all the hidden things of God is not yielding or believing in the purpose of God. However, God specifically held back the things of the future that we cannot understand. What we have is enough for now.

**"I Therefore, the prisoner of the Lord, beseech you that ye walk worthy of the vocation wherewith ye are called," (KJV, Eph. 4:1).**

Paul believed that no word in Scripture carried a more profound meaning than the word "Worthy" coupled with the word "Walk." Can we not agree it is the standard by which we seek the flag of obedience to Christ Jesus? It is a saying which the heathen is unable to ignore.

It ignites a vision of humility that is opposite to pride. Meekness is the excellent disposition of the soul. It defines a person called by God as one who is unwilling to provoke or offend. A self-evaluation of one's inner truth reveals the uneasy acceptance that we are not different from those in life whom we have difficulty forgiving.

One writer put it this way. "The sense of the word 'calling' and the agency employed in calling us as seen through the 'Effectual calling that is the work of God's Spirit, whereby convicting us of our sin and which misery enlightens our minds in the knowledge of Christ, which renews our wills, He persuades and enables us to embrace Jesus freely.' Scripture reading is but one way of influencing the mind, therefore gaining a greater understanding of our calling as we walk worthy toward God, which is the pathway to His Kingdom. Many believe that the influence exerted, or rather the mode in which the Spirit of God acts within the human mind, is much debated; however, the debate itself is evidence of the knowledgeable influence directed on the human mind. We need to break this down for understanding. Is it by,

**1.** Moral persuasion: An appeal to morality.

**2.** Physical power: The amount of energy transferred or converted.

**3.** Act of Creation (1) The act of or process of creating. (2) The fact of being created or produced. **3.** Something into existence or created.

**4.** Allowing the mind to exert its proper powers in the right way, thus turning to God.

What is the proper method or channel employed? Is it our decision?

**"The wind bloweth where it listeth, and thou hearest the sound thereof, but canst not tell whence it cometh, and whither it goeth: so is every one that is born of the Spirit," (KJV, Jn. 3:8).**

Therefore, who can define it? It is no other than the precise workings of the Holy Spirit.

# CHAPTER 9

## THE ORDINANCES OF GOD'S CALLING

God's purpose for the design of the human body is inclusive of the purpose of spreading the Gospel message. Many believe that,

**1.** Preaching; probably more are called into the Kingdom by the exhortation of the Word by hearing it preached than any other means.

(a) God's great ordinance for the salvation of men.

(b) The pulpit has a higher advantage for acting on the mind than any other means of affecting people.

I The truths that are dispersed; the sacredness of the place; the peace and quietness of the sanctuary; and the appeals to the reason, the conscience, and the heart. It suited all to affect people and to bring them to reflection.

(d) The Spirit makes use of the word "preached," however, it is through a great variety of ways.

In my personal experience as a listener, teacher, and occasional preacher, I have found that the same truth can have different effects on different people, with some being impressed and others not moved. In my personal experience as a listener, teacher, and occasional preacher, I have found that the same truth can have different effects on different people, with some being impressed and others not moved.

The positive side of the message is actually when the truth touches the heart of a sinner, after he may have heard it many times before without being moved to act upon it. The Holy Spirit provides the opportunity, and the message steps in and convicts the sinner to make a change.

The Spirit acts with sovereign power and by the laws that are never followed to their completion.

**2.** The events and/or actions of providence have been used to call many into God's Kingdom. He appeals to some by the use of pain, or by standing alongside a friend going through the heartache of mourning the loss of a loved one or even one who is at death's doorstep. The questions are many, as a friend of mine diagnosed with ALS is questioning what happens after death. Many turn against God in anger; yet, others come to Him and find peace.

**3.** Conversations for many have led them to Christ and they heed the calling of God. Therefore, they will one day enter the Kingdom of God. Some say this is the state of mind wherein the Spirit of God has prepared the soul like a farmer who prepares the ground for planting seeds. A brief conversation or a remark will trigger action rather than preaching.

4. Reading the Scripture is one of the more popular methods of calling lost souls into the Kingdom. The Word of God is the supreme means of harvesting the fields of lost souls. Sometimes getting a person to read anything is a challenge, yet when the Spirit has prepared the groundwork, most cannot put the Word of God down and become like a sponge soaking up the victory message of salvation.

**5.** It is in an unseen manner the Spirit calls people to the Kingdom of God. You may say He is responsible for and directs a person who may be examining his or her mental abilities. It was a movie about the end times that did this for me. The Holy Spirit flipped the light on in my brain and lit up my heart. My past suddenly came alive in my thoughts and I knew I had wasted my life on temporal pleasures. My conscience was overwhelmed with guilt at the thought of how I may influence my children before they enter adulthood.

The sinner will find him or herself reflecting on death, judgment, and eternity. That is the effect of the Holy Spirit of God working on the mind and leading a sinner to seek salvation answers. It is not by force; nor by violation of any laws, but by the moral law that a mind travels.

## PERSONAL STUDY NOTES

### WHAT HAVE I LEARNED

# CHAPTER 10

## BELIEF IN CHRIST, WHAT IT IS TO ME

1. It is to boldly profess our belief in Christ in all places, companies, employment, and any public domain. We are not to be Christian by name only or just on Sunday. Proclaiming our witness covers all aspects of our life, including the communion table, our place of residence, and anywhere the Lord may lead. The prompting of the Holy Spirit ignites the timing, and it may come at any moment and in the strangest places. Only fear will prevent a person from sharing the Gospel of Christ. Jesus said in John 16:33 "Fear not, for I have overcome the world. One writer put it this way: "Our calling as Christians places us in the counting room as well at the communion table and lest we not forget among strangers or when we are in a foreign land." The simple truth is that our starting point begins when we step through our front door into the wilderness world of lost souls.

**2.** Is it not inconsistent with the mature Christian character to do nothing? Is it permissible to give no thought to emotions or motives, and use no language to perform deeds that are inconsistent with the most mature Christian character? Is my silence dwelling among the lost condemning them to Hell, and should I not be concerned?

Jesus' death on the cross was not a guilt trip for us, the believers, to go out into the world and reluctantly share the Gospel of salvation. We are to share in joyful expressions the eternal salvation of Christ's sacrifice on the cross, and His rising from the grave to defeat spiritual death. Folks, that is our calling, and should that not also be our most earnest expectation as a convert to Christianity?

The cults are in high gear racing to claim the lost souls for the devil. We are in the last days and it appears the "Church" is stuck in the low-range gear; we need to shift gears and run the race to be victorious. Second place is not an option in sharing the Gospel with those who have not heard the "TRUE Gospel" of Christ. Not the doctored version, "You can work your way to Heaven or God will make you wealthy if you just accept Him and send in money to support this ministry or that ministry," or any other religion based on works or overbearing rules and regulations of traditions. Salvation is FREE!

Ask yourself, what does it mean to me to be called a Christian? It is a simple question, yet boils down to a heartfelt desire for choice. Either you are with Him or against Him. Watch this; Jesus aims this arrow directly at the center of one's heart.

**"He that is not with me is against me; and he that 0gathereth not with me scattereth abroad," (KJV, Matt. 12:30).**

Jesus' ministry up to Matthew 12 is about His proclaiming the good news. Chapter 12 is a pivotal point in His ministry. His message is now rejected—particularly by the Jewish leadership. The situation that triggered the claim in verse twelve came after Jesus healed a blind and mute man. Tribulation from arrogant nonbelievers comes in the form of hate and disrespect. When you share the Gospel, it may surprise you if it causes discontent. It simply means the reaction is normal for those who are not prepared to hear the Good News of Christ. However, it is a seed planted and we are to shake off the rejection and move on, allowing God to prepare the person's heart and mind. Not every person Paul came in contact with accepted the Gospel of Christ. We may never know the outcome of our sharing the message of the cross until we arrive in Heaven. Guilt is a tool of the devil.

**3.** Should we not do right, walking just as a witness to all encounters? It is a tough chunk of leather to chew on because we are human, which comes with emotions and temporal desires of the human heart and mind. Tell the truth: defend the Gospel and do not defraud others; maintain a correct standard of morals; to be known as an honest person steps on the worldly values of the heathen who does not know Christ or His message of salvation, and shocking as it may sound, some of those are in the Body of Christ calling themselves believers.

The correct standard of character and conduct for the Christian heart should be a heart that so lives such a life, that we may always know exactly where such a person stands when we look in the mirror. Who do we find looking back at us? A person should live as having no matter what others may believe or act toward such a person. That person's purpose is to be the unflinching advocate of temperance, chastity, honesty, and of every good work of every plan that is suited, alleviates human woe, and benefits a dying world.

Jesus did His part on the cross; He forgave sins for those who believe. Those who reject Him are the followers of the devil or children of the devil as Christ called them. Free will is a tool of both good and evil. Choice has but two roads, one ends in Heaven and the other in Hell.

**4.** Should we not live as one who "expects" to be in Heaven? How should such a person feel knowing that the earth is temporary and not his last home? Is that leather strip you are chewing on getting stuck in your teeth yet? Are we, not pilgrims and strangers, as many believe? Jesus taught that worldly riches, honors, and pleasures are of comparatively little value or importance. Jesus taught that a man ought to watch and pray. Pray about what? you may ask. Glad you asked. A man who realizes that he is but a second from Heaven or Hell is a man who employs the feeling that he ought to be holy and not evil.

He who begins a new day on Earth feels that the end is close and he may be among the angels of God and the spirits of just men made perfect will feel the importance of living a holy life, and if being wholly devoted to the service of God, "Pure should be the eyes that are soon to look on the throne of God," and "Pure the hands that are soon to strike the harps of praise in Heaven," and "Pure the feet that are to walk the golden streets above." (Author unknown),

**"Being confident of this very thing, that he which hath begun a good work in you will perform *it* until the day of Jesus Christ," (KJV, Phil. 1:6).**

Our hope is in Jesus, and we are to be confident of it. Paul's mission was to glorify Christ in all things. May that be our mission as well as we await the return of our Lord Jesus Christ. Amen?

Ephesians 4:1-32 depicts the exhortations to our Christian duties that rest on our Christian privileges, as united in one Body, though varying in the graces given to the several members that we may come unto a perfect man in Christ.

According to the Greek order, "I beseech you, therefore, (seeing that such is your calling of grace, the first through third chapters) I the prisoner in the Lord (that is, imprisoned in the Lord's cause): What the world counted ignominy, he courts the highest honor, and he glorifies in his bonds for Christ, more than a king in his diadem. His bonds, too, are an argument that should enforce his exhortation. Paul, even though in bondage, his highest desire was to proclaim Christ as King and Savior. Is our highest desire the same as Paul's, to proclaim Christ as King and Savior?

## Personal Study Reflection Notes

### What Have I Learned?

# CHAPTER 11

## CHRISTIANS CALLING FOR UNITY

What should be the main purpose of the born-again Christian and his or her calling? To find the answer, we must look at the book of Ephesians.

***"There is*** **one body, and one Spirit, even as ye are called in one hope of your calling; One Lord, one faith, one baptism, One God and Father, who** *is* **above all, and through all, and in you all," (KJV, Eph. 4:4-6).**

To understand what God's purpose of His is calling to us may be, we must search for what God has called His new covenant people (The Church) and how they are to live out worthily the unity in Christ, which is expressed in early Christological character and creedal formulas that are Trinitarian. Ponder this truth; the high calling of Christ is not for individual accomplishments and recognition, but to be a team member serving the whole Body for the edification of all. That statement alone is enough to draw the ire of most liberal instructors. The aspects of these creedal formulas span from Pentecost to the Rapture. Therefore, are we endeavoring to secure the unity of the Spirit in the bond of peace? (Eph. 4:3).

There are seven points to consider within the above three verses which deal with the term "Christian Unity."

**1.** "One body" represents the total number of believers from Pentecost to the Rapture. Most Christian writers believe this is what they call the silent Church. I agree with that statement although there are some discrepancies, that all believers ought to be visible. It may not always be easy; however, part of our witness is being seen obeying the commandments of our Lord in humbleness, Amen.

**2.** "One Spirit" represents the Holy Spirit who many believe baptizes each believer into the Body of Christ. Now, watch, the work of the Holy Spirit is to unify believers in Christ. Folks, it is the unity that they entrusted the believer to keep. God entrusts us to keep the unity of the Body. The division is not unity; there is no love in the division.

**3.** "One hope" represents our calling and the goal we may set before all believers, either as individuals or as a whole. "It will take them out of this world into the presence of Christ," meaning it is the blessed hope to which we cling (see Titus 2:13).

**4.** "One Lord" represents a vision of Jesus Christ, and His Lordship over all believers, therefore, bringing into existence the unity of His Church. Jesus came to divide those of repentance from the non-repentant households (Luke 12:51; Matt. 10:34). Division is never about unity and sin creates a division of the heart. Therefore, a heart divided is a heart that beats in turmoil. Jesus desires that the Body of Christ (the Church) be united in one spirit, living in His grace as complete. The very essence of His Word is that we abide in Him, and He in us together in one Body, one baptism, and one Lord and Savior Jesus Christ (See Romans 15:5:6)

**5.** "One faith" represents the Body of truth, the preference to the apostles' doctrine (Acts 2:42). We birth division through denial. Therefore, there must be a substance, an anchoring point, for believers to cling to as one Body. That substance equals correct doctrine. Amen.

**6.** "One baptism" applies to the work of the Holy Spirit, representing real baptism. Now watch this. Ritual baptism is by water, which means it is a symbol of the real baptism of the Holy Spirit which made believers as one. Some may argue the point, however, Scripture is clear.

**7.** "One God and one Father" represents God's fatherhood of the believers. This may be a hard concept for some; however, God is not the Father of the unbelievers.

**"Jesus said unto them, 'If God were your Father, ye would love me: for I proceeded forth and came from God; neither came I of myself, but he sent me. Why do ye not understand my speech?** *even* **because ye cannot hear my word. Ye are of** *your the* **devil, and the lust of your father ye will do. He was a murderer from the beginning, and abode not in the truth because there is no truth in him. When he speaketh a lie, he speaketh of his own: for he is a liar, and the father of it," (KJV, Jn. 8:42-44).**

The Jews did not believe Jesus was the Messiah or that He and the Father were one. They, therefore, felt He was spewing blasphemy toward God. The term unbeliever means those who do not follow the teaching of Jesus Christ and/or reject Him. Therefore, there is little difference between those Jews then and now and no difference from any nonbeliever today. Since there is but one Father in Heaven, He is not the Father of unbelievers. Sonship can come only through Jesus Christ. The unity of believers produces a sharp distinction between believers and nonbelievers. He is the Father of all who are His regeneration. Now, watch this, in Ephesians 4:6 the Apostle Paul noted that this Father "is over all and through all and in all." Each of this verse's four references to "all" comes from the same Greek root word, "pas." The phrasing used by Paul covers all aspects that God could be sovereign over. There is no carved type image of a god or anything else being higher than Him. (See also Col. 1:15; Jn. 1:1-5).

**"In whom we have redemption through his blood,** *even* **the forgiveness of sins," (KJV, Col. 1:14).**

Redemption means it has set us free through His blood, which was shed for all on the cross. Let us be clear about this statement. Christ shed His blood for all of humanity. However, to be redeemed, one must accept this gift of eternal life through Jesus Christ. One must know they require salvation and forgiveness of sins, therefore, each individual must believe that Jesus died for them and was raised by God three days later, defeating spiritual death (Rom. 10:9-10). Hearing the Word and accepting the Word must accompany an action on our part. Repentance of sin depicts an action taken by an individual followed by a public confession through baptism. Baptism cannot bring salvation, however; baptism is an outward expression of an inward conviction. Believing in who Jesus was and why He came, why He was born of a virgin, and why he shed His blood on an old, rugged cross is not an effortless task for some. The word belief is a powerful action of the heart and one's heartfelt desire to make a change for whatever reason.

**"Who is the image of the invisible God, the firstborn of every creature?" (KJV, Col. 1:15)** (See also Rev. 3:14).

Dependence on worldly desires is but a temporal existence. It will not and cannot be eternal, and it will rot away one day, never remembered for any good accomplished in life. We are not to worship any of the creation of this life nor the material things that humanity desires to own or employ.

**"For by him were all things created, that are in heaven, and that are in earth, visible and invisible, whether *they be* thrones, or dominions, or principalities, or powers: all things were created by him, and for him: And he is before all things, and by all things consist," (KJV, Col. 1:16-17)** (see also Heb. 1:2; 2:10).

As Christians, our call to unity must reflect that which God has called the Body (Church) of Christ to live out in our lives not only as individuals but as one unit, one mindset reflecting a true heart for Jesus Christ. Unity depicts the mindset of one, all in accord with one belief. That belief ought to depict the mind of Christ and who He truly is.

**"And he is the head of the body, the church: who is the beginning, the firstborn from the dead; that in all *things* he might have the preeminence. For it pleased *the Father* that in him should all fullness dwell," (KJV, Col. 1:18-19)** (see also Rev. 1:5).

Six times in Colossians chapter one, the words "All things" or "all fullness" depict a version of a unity of one. It means, "All things on Earth or in Heaven."

We were all once alienated and enemies of God in mind and wicked works (verse 21) and now reconciled unto God through the blood of Jesus Christ. Now, for many in our post-ascension world, the Christian finds himself against various beliefs worldwide. If we were to examine everyday living under the microscope of God, what would He find deep within our hearts concerning other beliefs? I believe He might find hatred or contempt mixed with some sadness and disbelief.

We know, according to Scripture, God calls us to love our neighbor as we love ourselves and it does not say just other believers. To live in unity is inclusive of all peoples. I believe God calls us to live in harmony, together with everyone, regardless of beliefs and differences. God calls us to do all things in love. No doubt life can be messy when we scope out the depth of relationships, stress, and the hurt and destruction of anger from misunderstandings or selfish attitudes. The valley of these differences stretches like a river through lives worldwide. The list of 15 Bible verses below concerns the unity of the Body of Christ, for the believer, and/or the nonbeliever who is seeking answers to questions about the calling of God.

First Corinthians 1:10 speaks of no division.

**"Now I beseech you, brethren, by the name of our Lord Jesus Christ, that ye all speak the same thing, and *that* there be no**

divisions among you; but *that* ye be perfectly joined together in the same mind and in the same judgment," (KJV, 1 Cor. 1:10).

The Apostle Paul says, "I beseech you" meaning he is begging us in the name of our Lord Jesus Christ that it would unite us in thought and speech perfectly joined in the same mind. Are we perfectly together, joined in thought and speech in our ultra-modern body of Christ? No, we are not. There is division among the brethren, though, not in who Jesus is and why He came. However, like the Jewish leadership that went over and above the Law of Moses, adding to the Law restrictions which were never intended by God. Some claim they are of the Body of Christ today. Now, like the Jews, of the Old Testament who had taken a great deal of God's Word out of context to satisfy worldly influences. Some modern church organizations have gone beyond scriptural teachings to bring in worldly doctrines. Paul says we are to be <u>united, perfectly joined.</u> Some Organized religions are separating the Body of Christ because of non-biblical rules and regulations found in the Old Testament and applying them to the church today. We must baptize you to be saved; you must speak in tongues to be saved, you must attend a certain church to be saved, etc. or you must meet on Saturdays to be a child of God. When we move away from God's Word, taught by worldly liberal pastors and professors, then how can our thoughts Unite? Agree or disagree is a choice, however, allowing a person whose lifestyle is an abomination in the eyes of God to stand in the pulpit. There is no difference between the Hebrews assimilating into the godless ways of the Egyptians and the Church allowing teachers and leaders without a moral basis to preach from the pulpit for other reasons. We must accept the teachings. God's order of things began in the beginning. We cannot and should not infuse the Body of Christ with worldly thinking. The worldly scream tolerance, however, being tolerant and united in one thought, and being true to the Word of God as written by His Spiritually inspired writers leaves us little if any wiggle room.

**2.** Second Corinthians 13:1, speaks of restoration, peace, love, comfort, and unity.

**"Finally, brethren, farewell. Be perfect, be of good comfort, be of one mind, live in peace; and the God of love and peace shall be with you," (KJV, 2 Cor. 13:11).**

The Apostle is wrapping up his letter to his Corinthian brothers (and possibly sisters, depending on the translation). In this passage, as in other farewell letters, Paul shoots from the hip in a series of rapid-fire instructions, although he uses a warm tone and then follows it up with a blessing. When he says; to be perfect, he is saying to be mature, and peaceful (see Rom. 15:33; Heb. 15:33). Restoration of the Body covers a multitude of subjects. He says we should rejoice because God provides for every moment forever. If God believes we are worth fighting for, then should we not rejoice in His mercy and love? Is that not worth celebrating? The apostle repeats we should aim or strive for restoration. Now, watch this, it includes repentance from any present sin and a return to devotion fully to Christ. The apostle and his friends are doing just that, (2 Cor. 13:9.) Paul continues to exhort them to comfort each other, agree with each other, and live in peace. Folks, we have a responsibility to build each other up. We cannot have unity if we are tearing others down; it is not acting in the spirit of love (Col. 3:13). We must learn to exhort a godly tolerance for moving past issues that can divide and prevent unification in Christ. It was a major divisional factor in Corinth (1 Cor. 1:10-11; 2 Cor. 12:21).

**3.** Acts 4:32 speaks of unity in heart and mind.

**"And the multitude of them that believed were of one heart and of one soul: neither said any *of them* that aught of things which he**

**possessed was his own; but they had all things common," (KJV, Acts 4:32).**

This passage is clear, The multitude that believed were of one heart and one soul. Here the Apostle Luke revisits a subject he had introduced back in Acts 2:44-45: the sharing of possessions among the believers. According to verse 32, the community of Jerusalem believers shared their possessions. They did not claim it as their own. Back in the 60s, the hippy communes lived a similar lifestyle. Hippies rejected established institutions, criticized middle-class values, opposed nuclear weapons and the Vietnam War, embraced the aspects of Eastern philosophy, championed sexual liberation, and were often vegetarian and eco-friendly. They promoted the use of psychedelic drugs which they believed expanded one's consciousness. The older generation today is reaping the downside of those drugs. I grew up in the '60s and '70s; however, I never lived in a commune environment, but it acquainted me with many who did. Most were very common people and, more than anything, they wanted closeness with one another, which traditional society had abandoned. The communes attempted to equalize income among the cooperatives by joining several cooperatives together, especially for farming. Similar only to the sharing of possessions and being united in heart and soul were the Corinthian believers.

**4.** Ephesians 4:23, speaks of having a new attitude.

**"And be renewed in the spirit of your mind," (KJV, Eph. 4:23).**

We must renew the mind and the spirit of separation from what we once were before our conversion. We were all deceived by sin therefore; our attitude must go through revitalization if we are to continue moving forward and not slipping back into a sinful lifestyle. Believe me when I say it can happen if we let our guard down. Satan is there to tempt us. He knows our past and will use it via the eyes and ears to lure us back into sin's dirty closet Eph. 4:22. The transformation can only come through Christ (Eph. 2:8-9), for those who come to know Him as Lord and Savior (Eph 4:21).

The Apostle Paul often spoke of the importance of being renewed in one's thinking (Rom. 12:2; Col.3:10). There is an ongoing power in our relationship with Christ that we should not ignore (2 Cor. 4:16; Titus 3:5). The renewing of our spirit and mind daily is a vital action that helps protect us from Satan's ever-increasing attempts to divert our desire to share the Gospel.

Our relationship with Christ is our defense against sin.

**"For they that are after the flesh do mind the things of the flesh; but they that are after the Spirit the things of the Spirit," (KJV, Rom. 8:5).**

The message in this verse is short and simple. Timing is everything they say. Just at the right time, Christ died for the ungodly. It is rare to find anyone who would die for a righteous person, although, for a good person, maybe, however not very often. Now, watch how God reveals His love for us.

**"But God commendeth his love toward us, in that, while we were yet sinners, Christ died for us," (KJV, Rom. 5:8).**

The difference between the one who lives by the Spirit and those who live by the flesh is that the Spirit-led is earnestly seeking God's will for their life. Those who live by the flesh are seeking self-satisfaction as the flesh nature directs. God's best is that His intense love for us gave Him no other option than to give us the very best. And that is His Son, Jesus Christ, amen.

**5.** Galatians 3:28 speaks of all people in Christ as one.

"There is neither Jew nor Greek, there is neither bond nor free, there is neither male nor female: for ye are all one in Christ Jesus," (KJV, Gal, 3:28).

According to Paul, all believers are one in Christ Jesus. Galatians 3:23-28 is Paul's fervent appeal to the Galatians; He explains that the law had been the jailer that imprisoned humans until the coming of faith, which is the coming of Christ, the object of this faith. Verse twenty-eight depicts that in Jesus' mind, there is no difference because we who believe in Him are all as one in our belief.

**6.** John 13:35 speaks of believers being His disciples.

"By this shall all *men* know that ye are my disciples, if ye have love one to another," (KJV, Jn. 13:35).

Consider the term "Love" which our modern anti-god world tosses around the word as if it were fodder for the beast of sin. Jesus crosses over the boundary lines of blood kin to include his fellow man. "Love one to another" is an open door to fellowship. Jesus was no stranger to hostility. The Jews hated Him, yet, He continued to love them even though they would nail Him to the cross. To be a disciple of Christ, one must hold on to the teaching of Jesus and love one another like you. It means we are to love, even the unlovable. Jesus said, "Forgive them Father for they know not what they do."

**7.** Philippians 2:1-3 speaks of our joy made complete by being like-minded.

"If *there be* therefore any consolation in Christ, if any comfort of love, if any fellowship of the Spirit, if any bowels and mercies, Fulfil ye my joy, that ye be like-minded, having the same love, *being* of one accord, of one mind. *Let* nothing *be done* through strife or vainglory; but in lowliness of mind let each other esteem other better than themselves," (KJV, Phil. 2:1-3).

There is no glory in vainness and strife. Self-satisfaction leads to destruction through prideful ambitions centered on self-glorification. There is no like-mindedness, therefore, resulting in an incomplete or empty joy.

**8.** Philippians 2:3 speaks of not being selfish or of vain conceit, but having humility in the value of others.

**"*Let* nothing *be done* through strife or vainglory; but in lowliness of mind let each esteem other better than themselves," (KJV, Phil. 2:3).**

Vainglory is pride, pure. "Let nothing be done through strife." There is nothing wrong with having an opposing viewpoint in matters of church business. Paul is saying that we, as Christians, have a responsibility to be an active force as one body united in the effort to achieve the communal goal of expanding the Kingdom of God. How do we do that? Glad you asked. One writer put it this way. We build the Kingdom by following Christ's example. His demonstration of humility and servanthood serve as an example. There it is; do all things with the humility of Christ's example in the forefront of all matters. There is no humility and no unity in pride.

**"Pride *goeth* before destruction, and an haughty spirit before a fall," (KJV, Pro. 16:18).**

(See also Jer. 49:16). One who walks around with a mirror in his face is one who does not see the pitfalls in his path and, therefore, stumbles about in the darkness in all that he does. The open mouth of the beast of sinful temptation eagerly waits to devour and destroy those wandering in the darkness.

**9.** Acts 2:1 speaks of being in one accord, which does not mean riding around in a Honda, but gathering together in one place, as were the apostles at Pentecost.

**"And when the day of Pentecost was fully come, they were all with one accord in one place," (KJV, Acts 2:1).**

This is the point where the Holy Spirit comes as Jesus said He would, at the perfect time and perfect place not only establishing His presence in each individual permanently but equipping the Saints for one purpose and that was to spread the Gospel, meaning the spreading of the Good News of Jesus' salvation message. Jesus forgives sins, reconciling sinners to God. Jesus said the fields were ready for the harvest as long as they would harvest. The harvest will not end until the Master says it is done, and His appearance is on the last day of the harvest.

**10.** Ephesians 4:11-13, speaks of God equipping His saints for the work of the Kingdom to build up the unity of God's people.

**"And he gave some, apostles; and some, prophets; and some evangelists; and some, pastors and teachers; For the perfecting of the saints, for the work of the ministry, for the edifying of the body of Christ: Till we all come in the unity of the faith, and of the knowledge of the Son of God, unto a perfect man, unto the measure of the stature of the fullness of Christ,"(KJV, Eph. 4:11-13).**

(See also Acts 20:28; Phil.1:1). Edifying means building up, to equip; an action on our part during our dwelling here on planet Earth, that of which God matches our calling for His purpose. And His purpose is unification into a Body of one. It takes thousands of parts to make an automobile perform to the high standard of the designer. Our designer is God, and His standard is righteous perfection. Paul is not referring to the gifts which God has given to men. However, it is God who gave the gifts, not men. It is my belief Christ calls men of various gifts and has given them to the Church for the perfecting of the saints, the work of the ministry for edification, which the result is the full maturity of the Body of Christ.

The purpose of the Church in the world is the completion of itself so that it may grow up. (See also Eph. 3:5; Col. 12:10; Gal. 1:1, 12; Rom. 12:7; 1 Cor. 12:28-29; 1 Tim. 3:2). Acts chapter 2 depicts that the apostles have dedicated the work of evangelism not only to members of the clergy but also to others. We, the general members of the body of Christ, are the evangelists in that we are called to share the Gospel of Christ with the world, meaning out our front door. Each of us has a story of our calling, and God expects us to share that story with a lost soul. If they reject it then the job is done. Pray for them and move on to another. We are not to badger a person into accepting Jesus as their Savior. If it does not come from the heart, it is not real. Many are not prepared to hear the Gospel of Jesus; however, a seed planted is a future flower of salvation. All believers need to be trained in the Word of God for the work of the ministry.

**11.** Colossians 3:13-14 speaks of forgiveness.

**"Forbearing one another and forgiving one another, if any man have a quarrel against any: even as Christ forgave you, so also *do* ye. And above all these things *put on* charity, which is the bond of perfectness. And let the peace of God rule in your hearts, to the which also ye are called in one body; and be ye thankful," (KJV, Col. 3:13-15).**

(See also Matt. 6:14; Rom. 13:8). Quarrel is a complaint. The apostle is referring to situations where there is blame involved and a complaint is justified. First, they should seek Christ in all situations. Having sound teaching at the forefront of thought says, "Even as Christ forgave you, so also do ye." It means that when we have a complaint against someone, we are to go to that person and seek common ground via forgiveness. That is the way to work out the issue. We are not to allow others to step all over us, but we are to handle situations through the wisdom of God's Word. It is an exhortation to put off the old man and put on Christ, (Col. 3:1). Sometimes situations arise where we encounter roadblocks and cannot find a solution because of the sinful nature of the world. In Luke 11:37-54, Jesus denounces the Pharisees. There was no forgiveness, and He just denounced them. Notice also that they did not seek forgiveness. Christ went to the cross to forgive us of our sins. Should it not be the example we base our forgiveness of our trespassers? "Above all things put on charity, which is the bond of perfectness." Charity is "love" in its purest form. Verses 13-15 contain two fruits of the Spirit-"Love and peace." And let the peace of God rule. The rule means to "umpire" meaning the peace of God should govern our hearts and we should be thankful.

**12.** John 17:23 speaks of complete unity in love.

**"I in them, and thou in me, that they may be made perfect in one; the world may know that thou hast sent me, and hast loved them, as thou hast loved me," (KJV, Jn. 17:23).**

"I in them, and thou in me." Seven words of the magnificent wonder that only the Spirit God Himself can accomplish. It depicts the unity that exists between the Father and the Son meaning the unity that is to exist between the believer and the Lord Jesus Christ. To think of the depth of that relationship with our lord boggles the mind! Is that not Heaven with Him in perfect fellowship?

**13.** Psalm. 133:1 speaks of the goodness and the joy of unity.

**"BEHOLD, how good and how pleasant *it is* for the brethren to dwell together in unity," (KJV, Psa. 133:1).**

(See also Gen.13:8). "To dwell in unity" Are believers not called to endeavor, to "keep the unity of the Spirit in the bond of peace?"(Eph. 4:3). My Bible says believers are one in Christ, meaning we are not to have our exclusive little group of busybodies.

Unfortunately, the Body of Christ all over the world includes such groups. Would it not be more beneficial for the Body of Christ to dwell together in a unity of oneness in Christ? Splinters can be painful and can cause infections. Having various splinter groups is infectiousness that leads to splits in the Body of Christ.

**14.** Ephesians. 4:1-6. Speaks of living a life worthy of our calling.

**"I THEREFORE, the prisoner of the Lord, beseech you that ye walk worthy of the vocation wherewith ye are called, With all lowliness and meekness, with longsuffering, forbearing one another in love; Endeavouring to keep the unity of the Spirit in the bond of peace. *There is* one body, and one Spirit, even as ye are called in one hope of your calling; One Lord, one faith, one baptism, One God and Father of all, who *is* above all, and through all, and in you all," (KJV, Eph. 4:1-6).**

(See also Col. 3:14). In verse 1, of Ephesians 4, the word "therefore" is what some call a connective, a transitional word that depicts the view of all that God has done for the believer, which the first three chapters of Ephesians cover. Paul calls himself a "prisoner of the Lord." As a witness for Christ, furthermore, Paul says he is a prisoner in his position in Christ, and that he could sit in the heavenly in Christ, yet sit in prison because he is a witness called by the Lord for the benefit of the Gentiles.

He says, "I beseech you, (I beg you) that you walk worthy wherewith the vocation you were called." It is a gentle form of the wooing of love (Rom. 12:1). Let our life be the witness of our walk of worthy calling as one in Christ (Phil.1:27; Col. 1:10; 1 Thess. 2:10; 1 Jn. 1:7). Verse 2 says. "With all lowliness and meekness and long-suffering, forbearing one another in love." Lowliness is the opposite of pride. We are not to walk in pride but walk in a worthy humbleness of mind. One writer said that "Lowliness is the flagship of Christian virtues." (Phil. 2:3; Matt. 11:29). Was he right? Yes. Long-suffering means a long temper. It is a fruit of the Spirit. (Read Gal. 5:22; Col. 3:13 for further study). Endeavoring to keep the unity of the Spirit and the Lord Jesus prayed that we be as one (John 17:21). Verse 4 says, "One body and one Spirit called in one hope." One body refers to the total number of believers from Pentecost to the Rapture. Some writers call this the invisible church. "One Spirit" refers to the Holy Spirit, who baptizes believers into the Body of Christ. "One hope" refers to our calling as believers and the goal set before all believers as the Body, which is the one that will leave this world and go into the presence of Christ. (See also Titus 2:13). "One faith" refers to the Body of truth called the apostles' doctrine (See Acts 2:42).

Now watch this: when humanity denies this doctrine, it results in divisions. It formed the correct substance of this doctrine in the adhesion of believers. Amen. "One baptism" refers to the real baptism of the Holy Spirit; ritual baptism is by water which is the symbol of real baptism. "One God and Father of all" refers to the only fatherhood of God for the believers. He is the Father of all who are His by regeneration.

**15.** First Peter 3:8 speaks of being sympathetic and like-minded in love and compassion.

**"Finally, *be ye* all of one mind, having compassion one of another, love as brethren, *be* pitiful, *be* courteous," (KJV, 1 Pet. 3:8).**

(See also Rom. 12:16). This is sound doctrine, though hard to live by in our ultra-modern "I serve myself" mentality. Being courteous or compassionate toward others is almost an ancient form of niceness. A practice seldom seen on Earth today and the portion of humanity that still holds to such actions is rightly condemned. What will Jesus find when He returns? Will He find faith, compassion, and kindness? We see a major move to divide and remove morality for evil and filth as the desired lifestyle. Self-preservation loaded with fleshly action is becoming the norm. One must ask, how much longer will the Lord tarry? (Habakkuk 1:1-11).

Some find this passage difficult to understand. However, in verse 2, the question many ask today is why must Christians suffer. This passage is a great example of many events happening today. The question posed is "Why doesn't God do anything about any particular situation?" Is there not a temptation for humanity to pray as though man controls the will of God or His plan? The simple truth is nobody controls the Almighty. This passage deals with the disobedient nation of Judah. God is not accountable to anyone. The truth of God's word is provided for our learning what not to do.

Why does God tolerate wickedness and injustice in His church or any nation of people Christian or non-Christian? God wishes that none shall perish, (2 Peter 3:9). Therefore His Grace, His mercy, and His great promises through Jesus His only Son provide a way to escape the coming destruction, (Romans 10: 9-11).

The great question for you and me is, "What are our expectations concerning the second coming of Christ?

## YOUR THOUGHTS

## PERSONAL STUDY NOTES

## WHAT HAVE I LEARNED

# CHAPTER 12

## HOW LONG LORD?

"The burden which Ha-bak'-kuk the prophet did see. O LORD, how long shall I cry, and thou wilt not hear! *Even* cry out unto thee *of* violence, and thou wilt not save! Why dost thou shew me iniquity, and cause *me* to behold grievance? For spoiling and violence *are* before me: and there are *that* raise up strife and contention," (KJV, **Hab. 1:1-3**). (See also Lam.3:8; Jer. 15:10.

Verses 1-11 refer to the problem the prophet exposes for us in verse 2 and follows it with: "How long, O LORD, must I call for help, but you do not listen?" What is he describing here? The exposing of the discrepancy between revelation and experience. How can we reconcile what we know of the character and purpose of a good and powerful God with all that we see around us? This is what the prophet is asking; this is the same question many today are asking. I have heard this argument all my life. "How can it possibly be that you, O God, are good and powerful, and yet violence and moral ineptitude and chaos confront us at every point?"

Look around at our nation over the last year. Do we have a collapsing economy, diminishing productivity, food shortages, violence, and social injustice, not to mention a wholesale disregard for God's law? What does that small list of everyday things conjure up in your mind? Does it say to the reader, "Well, maybe this just isn't as far removed from where we live as we thought?" Maybe the first 5 issues add up to a wholesale disregard for what God has said all along in His Word. Many believers see this problem as what it is. When we look at the whole of verses 1-11, we will see a twofold problem; God's timescale. Do we have the right to question God on His time-line?

Verse 2: "How long" is this going to go on? And God's tolerance, verse 3: "Why do you make me look at injustice?" We can toss in "Why do you tolerate wrong?" Some may believe it is a simple contemporary question. I lean toward a yes answer, meaning it is a question from the lips of every thoughtful believer, is it not? So many today question the goodness of a loving and moral God. The simple truth is we serve a God of tolerance toward archaic, spiritual, and moral dry rot amongst those who profess to be followers of His Son. Do we not need to look in the mirror and make it clear to ourselves that the history of Habakkuk's era was under God's control, and that it is true at every age that followed?

Have we not come full circle per se in our learning that the events of our modern world somehow relate to events of Habakkuk's day? Are they all tied together in their significance to God's eternal purpose relating to His Kingdom? Folks, maybe the confusion of our misunderstanding of the events on Earth, is not from God, but from whom we center our focus. Scripture tells us that our focus ought to be on the Son of God and that sharing the Gospel with a lost and dying world is far more beneficial than what we might perceive to be a major issue in our daily lives.

Habakkuk had seen a national revival, yet danger loomed ahead because of a national spiritual decline. His prophecy of the coming judgment on Judah weighed heavily on His mind and soul. Remember that every word of God for His children arrives with the heaviness of meaning and relevance.

The name Habakkuk comes from the Hebrew verb "embrace." Some believe his name means he who embraces or he who clings. One writer put it this way. It is an appropriate name for both the prophet and the book because Habakkuk comes to a firm faith through tough questions.

Both Christians and non-Christians grapple with tough questions and various situations during their lifetime. I do not believe it was ever different for the prophets of old because God has a purpose for this planet and its inhabitants. Although not confirmed, some believe that Habakkuk made his living by telling prophecies about the temple. Are we not plagued with modern-day self-proclaimed prophets and prophetesses who gather a good income in the prophecy business? God will one day clear it all up and I, for one, will steer clear of celebrity/social prophets and preachers who preach for monetary purposes.

Our earnest expectations should be in alignment with the Lord's plan as written in Scripture. We humans stray from our course when we attempt to put human thoughts in God's mind. I say attempt because that is all it can be. God's Word never changes and neither will His purpose and plan.

Are not our lives full of twists and turns? Are not the roads we travel daily filled with unexplained events? We start the day with a plan, yet along the way, we ask ourselves why this or that happens. None of us are above making a choice that we later regret. It is human nature, meaning the spontaneous actions activated by temptation and/or maybe a reaction to another's actions. Is not our faith tested in those moments when we must face choices we never planned or wanted to make? Grappling with choices or circumstances caused by spontaneous events that may catch us off guard happens more often than not. This is the point where the believer has the Holy Spirit available to step in and bring calmness to an uncertain situation that requires clear thinking.

The Holy Spirit reacts when allowed to do so. Believers are not above pushing past the Holy Spirit's advice to engage in a heated moment of human emotions or actions. Now, afterward, a believer may find himself or herself questioning God's reason for not stepping in. I know; because I have worn those shoes and it is not a pleasant feeling when the truth reveals to my stubborn nature that I should have heeded the caution sign flashing in my brain saying "Stop! Stop!" when I was young I remember watching *Lost in Space* and the robot telling the young actor, "Danger, Will Robinson, Danger." The Holy Spirit is like that robot in that He is yelling "Danger, Danger ahead!" We may find ourselves in the same position as King David.

**"How long, O LORD? Will you forget me Forever? How long will you hide your face from me? How long must I wrestle with my thoughts and every day have sorrow in my heart? How long will my enemy triumph over me?" (New International Version, Psa. 13:1-2).**

King David's heart and soul are in distress. He is pursuing answers from his Holy God because he believes God has turned His face against him. God never leaves us and the only time we turn His face against us is when we willfully sin, for He cannot look upon it. A change of attitude has come for King David in Psalm chapter 45, and in chapter 46, we see the message for us as believers shining like a beacon of light on a dark and stormy sea of confusion and doubt.

**"GOD is our refuge and strength, a very present help in trouble," (KJV, Psa. 46:1).**

My earnest expectations as a believer are that Christ Jesus is returning and when He comes, the cleansing of planet Earth will begin. The prophets of old have written about it and many modern-day pulpits are saying it is soon. Our duty as Christians is to share the Gospel of Christ with the world,( Acts 1:8, and Matthew 28:19-20), and when we share the Gospel, we are to reveal the conversion process (Romans 10:9-10). Many will continue to reject the Gospel, it is at that point our job is to turn them to God; we are in the clear. Ask the Lord to place another in your path to share the Good News with and pray that God has prepared that person's mind and heart to receive the message of salvation.

**"O CLAP your hands, all ye people; shout unto God with the voice of triumph," (KJV, Psa. 47:1).**

Rejoice; rejoice for the Lord of all creation has triumphed over evil, make straight your path, oh people of the Utmost High God, and hide His law in your heart and have rest in your soul for the Lord Jesus has come and has brought salvation through His blood and defeated death by His rising from the grave. Rejoice; rejoice, rise all you lowly hearts, and drink from the river of life Jesus Christ.

It Is my earnest expectation and hope that those who study and read the Holy Scripture will find rest and hope in our Lord and Savior Jesus Christ. This book is but a portion of my journey after I received Jesus into my life in the summer of 1980. Though I continue to fight the temptations of this evil and corrupt world, I know my destination after the last breath will be glorious and my fight against the flesh will end. My prayer is that somehow you, the reader, will learn something new from these words.

Jesus said, "I am the way, and the truth, and the life." He is the only road that leads to Heaven, Amen.

**"That if thou shalt confess with thy mouth the Lord Jesus, and shalt believe in thine heart that God hath raised him from the dead, thou shalt be saved. For with the heart man believeth unto righteousness; with the mouth confession is made unto salvation. For the scripture saith, Whosoever believeth on him shall not be ashamed. For there is no difference between the Jew and Greek: for the same Lord over all is rich unto all that call upon him. For whosoever shall call upon the name of the Lord shall be saved," (KJV, Rom. 10:9-13).**

Salvation cannot come from any other source but from Jesus Christ.

**"For God so loved the world, that He gave His only begotten Son, that whoever believes in Him should not perish but have everlasting life. For God did not send His Son into the world to condemn the world, but that the world through Him might be saved," (NKJV, Jn. 3:16-17).**

**"Jesus saith unto him, 'I am the way, the truth, and the life: no man cometh unto the Father, but by me,'" (KJV, Jn. 14:6).**

We have a direct link to the Father in Heaven. No baptism, priest, bishop, neither pastor, church nor any amount of good works, etc. can save us. Salvation comes from confession and belief. (Rom. 10:9-11). It is having faith in Jesus Christ the Son of God and through Him alone that we are saved.

# INVITATION

If you have not asked Jesus into your heart, then now is the time. Salvation is free.

"Jesus, I know I am a sinner. I know that I need a Savior. Please forgive me for my sins. I believe You died on the cross for me, a sinner, and that God raised You three days later so that I may have eternal life and dwell with You in Heaven. Cleanse my heart, Oh God, and renew a right Spirit within me." AMEN.

If you earnestly prayed that prayer to Jesus, then welcome to the family of God. Now find a local Body of true believers and get baptized as the public confession of your new faith in Jesus.

**How Do I Apply**

**What Have I Learned?**

# ABOUT THE AUTHOR

R.D. Millus also known as Randy lives on a large farm/ranch operation near Glenns Ferry, ID. Along the Snake River. He and his wife, Anna Marie, of 31-plus years, say that living in this area provides multiple opportunities to enjoy God's creation. The hunting, fishing, and wildlife are in abundance and allow Anna Marie (a published author, and wildlife photographer) ample opportunities to capture on film large herds of elk, deer, antelope, and various birds including large flocks of bald eagle and many pheasants, geese, and ducks, along the Snake River and on the ranch. He says moose, bear, mountain lion, and wolves have visited the ranch. Randy believes God has blessed them in abundance. Randy and Anna are active in their church. Randy is active in the local Trail Life USA Troop at First Baptist Church.

Other books by this author include The Gospel of John, Flesh and Bone, My Conscience and Me, Christian Liberty-Creation and Service to God, and just published The Wyoming Seaman along with his first mystery The Stranger on the Sidewalk, available on Amazon.

# BIBLIOGRAPHY

Accuracy and reference material consulted.

Holy Bible, Authorized King James Version, Thomas Nelson Publishers 1976

Holy Bible 500th Anniversary Edition, Authorized King James Version, Family Circle Edition; International Bible Press, the John C. Winston Co. 1944.

My Utmost for His Highest, Oswald Chambers Discovery House Publishers 1992

Everything Jesus Taught, Herbert Lockyer, Harper & Row Publishers 1976, 1984

Hebrew-Greek Study Bible, New International Version, Zodhiates, AMG Publishers 1996

Unger's Bible Dictionary, Moody Press, 1957, 1961 and 1966

Strong's Exhaustive Concordance of the Bible, Dr. James Strong, LL.D., S.T.D. Thomas Nelson Publishers 1990

Nave's Topical Bible, Orville J. Nave, A.M. D.D., LL.D. Baker Book House Publishers 1986

The Communicator's Commentary on Romans, D. Stuart Briscoe, Lloyd J. Ogilvie General Editor, Word Books, Publisher, Waco Texas 1982

Dr. J. Vernon McGee, Through the Bible Radio Program

Pastor Adrian Rogers, Radio Program "Love Worth Finding" https://www.lwf.org

www.ingramcontent.com/pod-product-compliance
Lightning Source LLC
Chambersburg PA
CBHW040937110426
42739CB00027B/52